Baking
with Mary Berry

Baking
with Mary Berry

First American Edition, 2015
Published in the United States
by DK Publishing
1450 Broadway Suite 801,
New York, NY 10018, USA

A catalog record for this book is available
from the Library of Congress.
ISBN 978 -1-4654-5323-5

DK books are available at special discounts
when purchased in bulk for sales
promotions, fund-raising, or
educational use. For details, contact:
DK Publishing Special Markets
1450 Broadway Suite 801,
New York, NY 10018, USA
SpecialSales@dk.com

Printed and bound in Canada

All images © Dorling Kindersley Limited
For further information see:
www.dkimages.com

A WORLD OF IDEAS:
SEE ALL THERE IS TO KNOW

www.dk.com

Contents

Introduction   6

Techniques   8

Breakfast foods   16
Flapjacks   18
French pancakes   20
Blueberry & vanilla muffins   22
White chocolate
  & strawberry muffins   24
Double-chocolate muffins   26
Zucchini loaf   27
Date & walnut loaf   28
Fruity banana bread   30
Apricot & cherry loaf cakes   31
Danish pastries   32

**Cakes, cupcakes
  & pastries**   34
Heavenly chocolate cake   36
Chocolate & beet cake   38
Devil's food cake   39
Chocolate & orange
  mousse cake   40
Pineapple & carrot cake   42
Simnel cake   44
Marbled coffee ring cake   46
Battenburg cake   48
Pineapple upside-down
  cake   49
Swiss roll   50
Fairy cakes   51
Chocolate cupcakes   52

Lemon cupcakes
  with lemon frosting   54
Coffee & walnut cupcakes   56
Cupcake tier   58
Baklava   60
Coffee éclairs   62
Religieuses   63
Chocolate profiteroles   64

**Cookies, bars &
  brownies**   66
Viennese fingers   68
Pinwheel cookies   69
Fridge cookies   70
Pecan & chocolate
  chip cookies   71
Gingerbread Christmas cookies   72
Almond tuiles   74
Ginger snaps   75
Brandy snaps   76
Shortbread   78
Pink almond macaroons   80
Coconut macaroons   82
Chocolate whoopie pies   83
Iced lime bars   84
Iced orange & lemon bars   86
Best-ever brownies   87
Gingerbread   88

Pies, tarts & cobblers   90
Mincemeat &
  almond tart   92
Strawberry & rhubarb pie   94

Royal raspberry tart	96
Double-crust apple pie	98
Tarte Tatin	100
French apple tart	102
Tarte au citron	104
French apricot & almond pie	106
Apple tarte au citron	108
Mississippi mud pie	109
Pecan pie	110
Lemon meringue pie	112
Key lime pie	114
Plum & almond tart	116
Raspberry tartlets	118
Tropical tartlets	119
Blueberry puffs	120
Apricot & almond galette	122
Mini apple, apricot &	
hazelnut crumbles	124
Classic apple crumble	125
Plum crumble	126
Blackberry & apple cobbler	128
Apple strudel	130

British favorites   132

Devon scones	134
Welsh cakes	136
Figgy seeded bites	137
Wimbledon cake	138
Victoria layer cake	140
Dundee cake	141
Treacle tart	142
Bakewell tart	144
Banoffi pie	146

Eve's pudding	148
Queen of puddings	149
Treacle pudding	150
Sticky toffee pudding	152
Christmas pudding	154
Steamed jam pudding	156
Magic chocolate pudding	158
Magic lemon pudding	160
Bread & butter pudding	162

Special occasion desserts   164

Cherry cheesecake	166
Rich fruit Christmas cake	168
Rich fruit cake	171
Hot chocolate soufflé	172
Summer berry soufflés	174
Twice-baked lemon soufflés	175
Pavlova with pineapple	
& ginger	176
Party pavlova pyramid	178
Pear & ginger pavlova	180
Hazelnut meringue roulade	
with berries	181
Strawberry meringue roulade	182
Ultimate chocolate roulade	184
Fresh fruit baskets	186
Choclate meringue shells	187
Mocha meringue mille-feuilles	188
Index	190
Acknowledgments	192

Introduction

As a judge on PBS's *The Great British Baking Show*, I am thrilled to share with you the recipes I bake at home—favorites for cakes, pies, bars, cookies, breakfast pastries, and desserts. All the recipes are foolproof and straightforward, and can be enjoyed on all kinds of occasions, as a simple treat for family and friends or to delight at celebrations and parties.

At home, I usually make the cakes, bars (we call them traybakes in England), and cookies for afternoon tea—yes we still have it! I love nothing more than the family and grandchildren coming over for tea and homemade cake. I bake with them too. My five grandchildren have all cooked with me from an early age and it is a joy now to see them baking for school events and parties.

So I hope you enjoy my recipes, too. Baking is such a joy—to do and to share.

Mary Berry

Techniques

Whisked cakes

Light, fatless cakes are raised by air whisked into eggs. Use a hand-held electric mixer or a large, table-top mixer. If using a hand-held mixer, set it at high speed.

1

Whisk the eggs, or egg yolks, with the sugar until the mixture is light, pale, and thick enough to leave a trail on the surface when the beaters are lifted out.

2

Gently fold in the flour and any other ingredients. If the eggs have been separated, the whisked egg whites should be folded into the mixture last of all.

All-in-one cakes

Be sure to use a soft butter for this quick, simple technique.

Put all the ingredients into a large bowl and beat together with a hand-held electric mixer until combined. You can also mix in a food processor or by hand.

Creamed cakes

The creaming method is used for both cakes and cookies. A wooden spoon, rubber spatula, or electric mixer are all suitable. Be sure to soften the butter or margarine first.

1

Cream the fat and sugar together until the mixture is pale in color and fluffy in texture. Keep scraping the sides of the bowl with a spoon or spatula to incorporate all of the mixture.

2

Lightly beat the eggs. Gradually add the eggs to the creamed mixture, beating well between each addition. If the mixture curdles, which will result in a dense-textured cake, beat in a spoonful of the flour.

3

Sift in the flour and any other dry ingredients. Using a wooden spoon, gently fold in the flour until well-combined. Any liquid ingredients should also be added at this stage.

Preparing cake pans

Lightly greasing the pan ensures a cake will turn out easily. Some recipes also call for the pan to be floured or lined with parchment paper.

Greasing and flouring
Use melted or softened butter, margarine, or oil, according to the recipe. Brush over the bottom and sides of the pan using a pastry brush or paper towels. If flouring, add a spoonful of flour and tilt the pan to coat it with a thin layer. Pour out any excess flour.

1

Lining
Set the cake pan on a sheet of parchment paper and mark around the base with a pencil or the tip of a knife.

2

Cut out the shape, cutting just inside the line, then press smoothly over the bottom of the pan. Lightly grease if directed in the recipe.

Baking, testing, and cooling cakes

Before baking cakes, breads, and cookies, be sure to preheat the oven to the correct temperature.
If you need to, adjust the position of the oven racks before you turn on the oven.

1

As soon as the mixture is prepared, pour it into the pan and level the surface. Tap the pan on the work surface to break any large air bubbles. Transfer immediately to the oven.

2

When cooked, a cake will shrink slightly from the sides of the pan. To test, lightly press the middle with a fingertip; the cake should spring back. Rich cakes should feel firm to the touch.

3

Set the cake pan on a wire rack and let cool for about 10 minutes. Run a knife around the sides of the cake to free it from the pan.

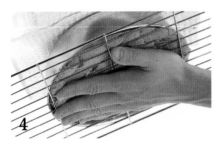

4

Hold a wire rack over the top of the pan, then invert the rack and pan so that the cake falls onto the rack. Carefully lift the pan away from the cake.

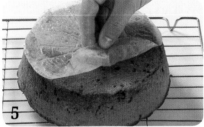

5

Peel off the lining paper. With a light-textured cake, turn it over again so the base is on the rack; this will prevent the rack from marking the top.

6

To cut the cake in half, steady it by setting one hand gently on top. Cut the cake horizontally, using a gentle sawing action.

Filling and frosting cakes

There are many simple ways to fill or decorate cakes. Whipped cream, jam, or chocolate spread make quick and easy fillings. Buttercream frosting can be made in a variety of flavors, to complement the flavor of the cake.

Chocolate buttercream frosting

Beat together 10 tbsp softened butter, ¼ cup cocoa powder, and 2 cups sifted confectioners' sugar. Add a little milk if necessary to give a spreading consistency. For a citrus frosting, omit the cocoa powder and add finely grated orange or lemon zest.

Spreading frosting

Only frost a cake when it has cooled completely. Use a large palette knife and spread the frosting with long, smooth strokes over the top and sides of the cake. Dip the palette knife in warm water if the frosting sticks to it.

Testing fruit cakes

For fruit cakes and other loaves, insert a metal skewer or long wooden toothpick into the middle: the skewer or toothpick should come out clean, without any moist crumbs sticking to it.

Shortcrust pastry dough

You can also make shortcrust in a food processor: pulse the flour with the fat until like bread crumbs, then add the water and pulse again briefly (do this briefly or the dough will be tough). Transfer to a floured surface and knead lightly to mix to a smooth dough. These quantities make sufficient dough to line a 9–10in (23–25cm) tart dish, tart pan, or pie dish.

1 Sift 1½ cups all-purpose flour into a bowl. Cut 6 tbsp well-chilled butter, margarine, or other fat into small pieces and add to the bowl. Stir to coat the fat with flour.

2 Using your fingertips, quickly and lightly rub the fat into the flour, lifting the mixture to incorporate air, until it resembles fine bread crumbs. Sprinkle over about 2 tbsp cold water and stir gently with a butter knife to mix. If the mixture seems too dry to bind together, add a little more water.

3 Gather the mixture together and knead very briefly until smooth (handle the dough as little as possible or it will be tough). If the dough feels at all sticky, add a little more flour. Shape into a ball, wrap, and chill for 30 minutes.

Pâte sucrée

This French sweet dough is traditionally made on a marble surface. These quantities make sufficient dough to line a 10in (25cm) tart dish, pan, or pie dish. For a less rich dough, use just 1 large egg yolk.

1 Sift 1¾ cups all-purpose flour onto a work surface. Make a well in the middle and add 6 tbsp softened butter, ¼ cup granulated sugar, and 3 large egg yolks. With your fingertips, blend together the butter, sugar, and egg yolks.

2 Using your fingertips, gradually work the sifted flour into the blended butter mixture until the mixture resembles coarse crumbs. If the mixture seems too sticky, work in a little more flour.

3 With your fingers or a pastry scraper, gather the dough into a ball, then knead briefly until it is smooth and pliable. Shape the dough into a ball again, wrap, and chill for 30 minutes or until it feels just firm.

Quick puff pastry

Ideal for both sweet and savory pies. These quantities make sufficient pastry for a 10in (25cm) double-crust pie.

1 Sift 2 cups all-purpose flour into a bowl. Add 6 tbsp each of cubed butter and white vegetable fat, and stir to coat in flour. Add ½ cup cold water and, with a butter knife, bind to a lumpy dough.

2 Roll out the dough into a rectangle 3 times as long as it is wide. Fold the bottom third up and the top third down. Press the edges with the side of your hand to seal. Wrap and chill for 15 minutes.

3 Roll out the dough into a rectangle and fold as before. Turn the dough so the folded edges are to the sides again. Repeat the rolling, folding, and turning twice more. Wrap and chill for 30 minutes.

Basic choux pastry

1

Put 4 tbsp butter, cut into cubes, into a heavy saucepan with ½ cup water and heat until the butter melts. Bring to a boil.

2

Remove from the heat and add ½ cups sifted all-purpose flour and a pinch of salt, if preferred. Stir vigorously until the mixture forms a soft ball.

3

Let cool slightly, then gradually add 2 lightly beaten large eggs, beating well between each addition, to form a smooth, shiny paste.

Making a pastry crust

Careful handling of pastry dough should ensure it does not shrink or distort when baking.

1

Put the pastry dough on a floured work surface and flour the rolling pin. Roll out into a round, starting in the middle each time and lifting and turning the pastry round a quarter turn after each roll.

2

If lining a pie dish, roll out the pastry dough to a round 2in (5cm) larger than the top of the dish; a pastry lid should also be 2in (5cm) larger. Roll the dough up loosely around the rolling pin, and unroll over the dish.

3

Gently ease the dough into the dish, pressing it firmly and neatly into the bottom edge. Be very careful not to stretch the dough. Carefully trim off the excess dough with a butter knife. If there are any holes, patch them with bits of dough.

Baking blind

A pastry crust may be partly baked before adding a filling, to help it stay crisp, or it may be fully baked if the filling itself does not need to be cooked. The dish is filled with baking beans to weigh it down.

1

Prick the pastry crust all over with a fork. Line with a piece of foil or parchment paper, allowing it to come high above the rim so that it can be lifted out easily after baking.

2

Fill the crust with ceramic baking beans, dried pulses, or uncooked rice, and bake in a preheated oven at 375°F (190°C) for 10 minutes.

3

Remove the beans and foil. Return the pan to the oven and bake for 5 minutes (part-baked) or 15 minutes (fully baked). If the dough rises during baking, gently press it down.

Shaping Danish pastries

1

2

Crescents
Roll out the dough into a 9in (23cm) round. Cut into quarters. Place a small roll of almond paste at the wide end of each piece.

Starting from the wide end, roll up each dough quarter loosely around the almond paste, then curve the ends to form a crescent.

Pinwheels and Envelopes
For pinwheels: roll out the dough and cut into 4 squares as for kites. Put almond paste in the middle of each. Cut from the corners almost to the middle. Fold in alternate points.

1

2

Kites
Roll out the dough into an 8in (20cm) square. Cut into 4 squares. Make cuts around 2 corners of each square, ½in (1cm) in from the edge.

Place a round of almond paste in the middle of each square. Lift each cut corner and cross it over the almond paste to the opposite corner.

For envelopes: roll out the dough, cut into 4, and fill as for pinwheels. Fold 2 opposite corners into the middle. Top with a half apricot, cut-side down.

Steamed puddings

Light cakes and rich suet mixtures can both be gently cooked by steaming. Be sure to make the seal tight so moisture cannot get inside. It is important to keep the water in the saucepan topped off, so boil some water ready to add to the pan when needed.

1

2

3

Turn the mixture into a greased, heatproof bowl. Layer a piece of parchment paper with a piece of foil and make a pleat across the middle, to allow for the pudding's expansion during cooking. Butter the paper.

Place the foil and paper, buttered-side down, over the top of the bowl. Secure by tying string tightly under the rim. Form a handle with another piece of string. Trim away excess paper and foil.

Put an upturned saucer or plate in the bottom of a saucepan and half fill with water. Bring to a simmer. Lower the bowl into the saucepan; add boiling water to come halfway up the sides of the bowl. Cover tightly and steam for the required time. Keep the water at simmering point and add more when necessary.

Crème pâtissière

1

Put 3 large eggs, ⅓ cup vanilla sugar, and ⅓ cup all-purpose flour into a large bowl, add a little milk taken from 1¾ cups, and mix until smooth. Pour the remaining milk into a heavy saucepan and bring almost to a boil. Pour onto the egg mixture, whisking well.

2

Rinse out the saucepan to remove any milk residue. Return the egg mixture to the pan, and cook over low heat, stirring continuously, until thickened.

3

Pour into a bowl and cover with plastic wrap, gently pressing it over the surface of the custard to prevent a skin from forming. Let cool.

Whisking egg whites

A balloon whisk is the classic tool for whisking egg whites, but an electric mixer saves time and effort. Ensure all your equipment is clean, dry, and grease-free, and that the egg whites are at room temperature.

Whisk the whites as forcefully as possible (on maximum speed if using an electric mixer) right from the start. When they look like a cloud, add any sugar little by little. The mixture will get stiffer and stiffer as you add sugar and whisk

Folding egg whites

To retain as much air as possible, egg whites should be folded gently and quickly into a mixture.

Mix a spoonful of the whites into the heavy mixture to lighten it. Using a rubber spatula or metal spoon, fold in the remaining whites using a "figure of eight" motion, cutting straight through the mixture, then turning it over until well blended.

Sauces for puddings

Hot chocolate sauce Heat 6oz (175g) dark chocolate, broken into pieces, 2 tsp instant coffee granules, ½ cup hot water, and ⅓ cup granulated sugar in a pan until the chocolate has melted. Serve hot.

Butterscotch sauce Heat 2 tbsp butter, ¾ cup light brown sugar, and ⅔ cup corn syrup in a pan until melted. Remove from the heat and add ½ cup heavy cream and a few drops of vanilla extract, stirring until smooth. Serve hot.

Chocolate marshmallow sauce Heat 2oz (60g) chopped dark chocolate, 1½ cups mini marshmallows, ⅓ cup heavy cream, and ⅓ cup honey in a pan until the chocolate and marshmallows have melted. Serve hot.

Sweet white sauce Blend together 3 large eggs, 2 tbsp granulated sugar, and 1 tsp of cornstarch. Heat 1¼ cups of milk to just below boiling and stir into the egg mixture. Return to the pan and heat gently, stirring, until thickened. Strain into a cold bowl to prevent further cooking, and serve warm or cold.

Breakfast goods

Flapjacks

 MAKES 24

Ingredients

9 tbsp butter, plus extra for greasing

¼ cup corn syrup

½ cup light brown sugar

2½ cups rolled oats

SPECIAL EQUIPMENT

baking dish, about 8 x 12in (20 x 30cm)

Method

1 Preheat the oven to 350°F (180°C). Lightly butter the baking dish.

2 Combine the butter, syrup, and sugar in a saucepan and heat gently until the ingredients have melted and dissolved. Stir in the oats and mix well.

3 Spoon into the prepared pan and smooth the surface with a palette knife. Bake for about 30 minutes.

4 Let cool in the pan for about 5 minutes, then mark into 24 bars. Let cool completely, then cut and remove from the pan.

French pancakes

 SERVES 4

Ingredients

**4 tbsp butter, softened,
plus extra for greasing**

⅓ cup granulated sugar

2 large eggs, beaten

½ cup self-rising flour

1¼ cups milk

**apricot jam and granulated sugar
to serve**

SPECIAL EQUIPMENT

8-hole muffin pan with 3in (7cm) cups

Method

1 Preheat the oven to 375°F (190°C). Combine the butter and sugar in a bowl and cream together until soft. Beat in the eggs, a little at a time, then fold in the flour.

2 In a small saucepan, heat the milk to just below boiling point. Stir into the creamed mixture.

3 Lightly butter the muffin pan cups, and divide the batter equally among them. Bake for about 20 minutes until the pancakes are well-risen and golden brown.

4 Slide the pancakes out of the cups and serve with apricot jam and granulated sugar. To eat, place a little jam in the middle of each pancake, fold in half, and sprinkle with sugar.

Blueberry & vanilla **muffins**

 MAKES 12

Ingredients

1¾ cups all-purpose flour

2 tsp baking powder

⅔ cup granulated sugar

¾ cup milk

1 tsp vanilla extract

2 extra large eggs

⅔ cup sunflower oil

3oz (90g) blueberries

SPECIAL EQUIPMENT

deep 12-hole muffin pan
and 12 paper liners

Method

1 Preheat the oven to 350°F (180°C). Line the muffin pan with the paper liners.

2 Put all the ingredients, except the blueberries, into a bowl. Beat with a hand-held mixer until evenly combined and smooth (it is quite a thin mixture). Stir in the blueberries.

3 Divide the mixture among the paper liners. Bake for 25–30 minutes until well-risen and light golden. Serve warm.

These are much loved by children. For a slightly more sophisticated touch, replace the white chocolate chips with dark chocolate chips.

White chocolate & strawberry **muffins**

 MAKES 12

Ingredients

2½ cups self-rising flour

⅔ cup granulated sugar

2 large eggs

1 cup milk

7 tbsp butter, melted

2 tsp vanilla extract

3½oz (100g) white chocolate chips

3 tbsp strawberry jam

confectioners' sugar, to dust

SPECIAL EQUIPMENT

deep 12-hole muffin pan lined with paper muffin liners

Method

1 Preheat the oven to 400°F (200°C). Put all the ingredients except the chocolate chips and jam into a large bowl and beat with a hand-held mixer until smooth. Stir in the chocolate chips.

2 Divide half the mixture evenly between the liners, spoon 1 teaspoon of jam on top of each one, then spoon the remaining mixture on top.

3 Bake for 25–30 minutes or until well-risen and lightly golden brown.

4 Dust with a little confectioners' sugar and serve warm or cold.

Double-chocolate muffins

For image see p53

 MAKES 12

Ingredients

2 large eggs, lightly beaten

½ cup full-fat plain yogurt

½ cup strong brewed coffee

½ cup milk

1¾ cups self-rising flour, sifted

1 cup granulated sugar

¾ cup cocoa powder

pinch of salt

3½oz (100g) chocolate chips

melted butter for greasing

SPECIAL EQUIPMENT

12-hole muffin pan

Method

1 Preheat the oven to 400°F (200°C). Combine the eggs, yogurt, coffee, and milk in a large bowl.

2 Sift together the flour, sugar, cocoa powder, and salt, and stir into the milk mixture. Mix well. Stir in the chocolate chips.

3 Butter each cup of the muffin pan, then spoon in the muffin mixture, filling the cups almost to the tops.

4 Bake the muffins for about 10 minutes; reduce the oven temperature to 350°F (180°C), and continue to bake for about 15 minutes until the muffins are golden and firm. Serve warm.

Zucchini **loaf**

 CUTS INTO 12 SLICES

Ingredients

½ **cup sunflower oil, plus extra for greasing**

8oz (225g) zucchini

2 large eggs

1 cup granulated sugar

¼ **tsp vanilla extract (optional)**

3 cups self-rising flour

1 tsp ground cinnamon

⅔ **cup walnut pieces, coarsely chopped**

SPECIAL EQUIPMENT

9 x 5in (23 x 13cm) loaf pan

Method

1 Preheat the oven to 350°F (180°C) and lightly grease the loaf pan. Coarsely grate the zucchini, put into a sieve, and leave for about 30 minutes to drain.

2 Beat the eggs until light and foamy. Add the sunflower oil, sugar, vanilla extract (if using), and zucchini and mix lightly until combined.

3 Sift the flour and cinnamon into a large bowl. Make a well in the middle, pour in the zucchini mixture, and stir to mix thoroughly. Stir in the chopped walnuts.

4 Pour the mixture into the greased loaf pan and bake for about 50 minutes until firm. Turn onto a plate and cool.

Date & walnut **loaf**

 CUTS INTO 12 SLICES

Ingredients

**6 tbsp soft butter or margarine,
plus extra for greasing**

**1½ cups dates, pitted
and coarsely chopped**

⅔ cup boiling water

½ cup granulated sugar

1 large egg

1¾ cups self-rising flour

1 cup walnuts, coarsely chopped

SPECIAL EQUIPMENT

9 x 5in (23 x 13cm) loaf pan

Method

1 Lightly grease the loaf pan with butter and line the bottom with parchment paper.

2 Put the dates into a bowl, pour in the measured boiling water, and leave for about 15 minutes. Preheat the oven to 350°F (180°C).

3 Combine the butter, sugar, egg, and flour in a large bowl and beat until well blended. Add the walnuts and dates, plus the soaking liquid, and stir to mix.

4 Spoon into the prepared loaf pan and bake for 1¼–1½ hours until well-risen and firm to the touch. A fine skewer inserted into the middle of the loaf should come out clean.

5 Let cool in the loaf pan for a few minutes, then turn onto a wire rack and peel off the lining paper. Let cool completely. Serve sliced and buttered, if wished.

Cherry and banana loaf

Omit the dates and walnuts and add 1 cup quartered glacé cherries and 2 mashed large, ripe bananas in step 3.

Fruity banana **bread**

 CUTS INTO 12 SLICES

Ingredients

9 tbsp butter or margarine, plus extra for greasing

1¾ cups self-rising flour

⅔ cup granulated sugar

¾ cup golden raisins

⅔ cup walnuts, coarsely chopped

1 cup glacé cherries, quartered, rinsed, and dried

2 extra large eggs, beaten

1lb (500g) bananas, weight with peel, peeled and mashed

SPECIAL EQUIPMENT

9 x 5in (23 x 13cm) loaf pan

Method

1 Preheat the oven to 325°F (160°C). Grease the loaf pan and line the bottom with parchment paper.

2 Put the flour into a bowl, add the butter, and rub in with your fingertips until the mixture resembles fine bread crumbs. Mix in the granulated sugar, golden raisins, chopped walnuts, and glacé cherries.

3 Add the eggs and mashed bananas and beat the mixture until well-blended. Spoon into the prepared pan.

4 Bake for about 1¼ hours until well-risen and firm to the touch. A fine skewer inserted into the middle of the loaf should come out clean.

5 Let the loaf cool slightly in the pan, then turn onto a wire rack and peel off the lining paper. Let the loaf cool completely before slicing and serving.

Small loaf cakes are always lovely to make and are quicker to bake than large ones. This recipe makes two. If you don't need both right away, you can eat one and freeze the other.

Apricot & cherry loaf cakes

 MAKES 2

Ingredients

8 tbsp butter, softened, plus extra for greasing

1½ cups self-rising flour

½ cup granulated sugar

3 extra large eggs, beaten

1½ cups dried apricots, sliced into small pieces

⅓ cup raisins

⅓ cup glacé cherries, sliced into small pieces

SPECIAL EQUIPMENT

two 5½ x 3in (14 x 8cm) mini loaf pans

Method

1 Preheat the oven to 350°F (180°C). Grease the loaf pans and line the bottoms and sides with parchment paper.

2 Put the flour, butter, sugar, and eggs into a mixing bowl and beat with a hand-held mixer until combined. Stir in the dried fruit and cherries, then spoon into the pans and level the tops.

3 Bake for 45–50 minutes or until golden brown and well-risen. Transfer to a wire rack to cool completely.

Danish pastries

 MAKES 16

Ingredients

3⅓ cups bread flour,
plus extra for dusting

½ tsp salt

26 tbsp butter, cut into small pieces,
plus extra for greasing

1 x ¼oz (7g) package fast-acting yeast

¼ cup granulated sugar

⅔ cup tepid milk

2 large eggs, beaten,
plus an extra to glaze

FILLING AND TOPPING

8oz (250g) white almond paste

4 apricot halves, canned or fresh

about 2 tsp water

1 cup confectioners' sugar

½ cup sliced almonds

½ cup glacé cherries

Method

1 Put the flour and salt into a bowl and rub in 4 tbsp of the butter. Stir in the yeast and sugar. Make a well in the middle, add the lukewarm milk and eggs, and mix to a soft dough.

2 Turn the dough onto a floured surface and knead for 10 minutes or until smooth. Shape into a round and place in an oiled bowl. Cover with oiled plastic wrap and leave in a warm place to rise for 1 hour or until doubled in size.

3 Turn the dough onto a lightly floured work surface and knead for 2–3 minutes until smooth. Roll out into an 8 x 14in (20 x 35cm) rectangle. Dot the top two-thirds of the dough with half of the remaining butter. Fold the bottom third up and the top third down to form a parcel. Seal the edges, then give the dough a quarter turn so the folded side is to the left.

4 Roll out the dough into an 8 x 14in (20 x 35cm) rectangle as before. Dot with the remaining butter, fold, and chill for 15 minutes. Roll, fold, and chill twice more.

5 Preheat the oven to 425°F (225°C). Divide the dough into 4 pieces. Shape and fill the pastries (see p14). Arrange on buttered baking sheets and let rise in a warm place for 20 minutes. Brush with beaten egg and bake for 15 minutes or until golden brown. Transfer to a wire rack.

6 Mix the water and confectioners' sugar and spoon a little over each pastry while still warm. Decorate kites with sliced almonds and pinwheels with glacé cherries. Let cool.

Cakes, cupcakes & pastries

Heavenly chocolate **cake**

 CUTS INTO 8 SLICES

Ingredients

9 tbsp butter, plus extra for greasing

7oz (200g) dark chocolate, broken into pieces

2 tbsp water

3 large eggs, separated

½ cup granulated sugar

½ cup self-rising flour

½ cup ground almonds

FUDGE FROSTING

9 tbsp butter

¾ cup cocoa powder

about 6 tbsp milk

4 cups confectioners' sugar, sifted

white chocolate curls to decorate

SPECIAL EQUIPMENT

deep 8in (20cm) cake pan

Method

1 Preheat the oven to 350°F (180°C). Lightly butter the pan and line the bottom with parchment paper.

2 Put the chocolate in a heatproof bowl with the butter and water. Place the bowl over a pan of hot water and heat gently, stirring, until the mixture has melted. Cool.

3 Combine the egg yolks and granulated sugar in a large bowl and beat together with a hand-held mixer until fluffy and very light in color. Stir in the cooled chocolate mixture. Carefully fold in the flour and ground almonds.

4 In a separate bowl, whisk the egg whites until stiff but not dry. Fold into the cake mixture, gently but thoroughly. Pour the mixture into the prepared pan. Bake for 50 minutes or until well-risen and firm to the touch.

5 Let the cake cool in the pan for a few minutes, turn onto a wire rack, and peel off the lining paper. Cool completely. Make the fudge frosting: melt the butter in a pan, add the cocoa powder, and cook, stirring, for 1 minute. Stir in the milk and confectioners' sugar. Beat well until smooth. Let cool until thickened.

6 Split the cake in half horizontally and sandwich the layers together with half of the fudge frosting. With a palette knife, spread the remaining frosting over the top and sides of the cake. Decorate with white chocolate curls.

Chocolate & beet **cake**

 CUTS INTO 8 SLICES

Ingredients

10 tbsp soft butter, plus extra for greasing

1 cup light brown sugar

3 extra large eggs

¾ cup cocoa powder

1½ cups self-rising flour

¼ cup milk

8oz (250g) cooked beets, peeled and coarsely grated

CHOCOLATE FUDGE FROSTING

4 tbsp butter

⅓ cup cocoa powder, sifted

3 tbsp milk

2 cups confectioners' sugar, sifted

SPECIAL EQUIPMENT

9in (23cm) springform or loose-bottomed cake pan

Method

1 Preheat oven to 350°F (180°C). Lightly grease the pan and line the bottom with parchment paper.

2 Combine all the cake ingredients, except the beets, in a large bowl. Beat with a hand-held mixer until smooth, then fold in the beets. Spoon the mixture into the prepared pan.

3 Bake for 45–55 minutes until the cake is well-risen and shrinking away from the sides of the pan. Set aside to cool a little, then remove the side of the pan (leaving the cake on the base), and let cool completely.

4 Make the frosting: melt the butter in a saucepan, add the cocoa powder, and stir over high heat for 1 minute. Add the milk and confectioners' sugar and stir to combine. Remove from the heat and set aside to cool and thicken.

5 Remove the cake from the base of the pan and peel off the lining paper. Using a serrated knife, slice the cake in half to make 2 equal layers. Spread one-third of the frosting on the bottom half and place the other half on top. Spread the remaining frosting over the top and side of the cake to give a thin layer. Serve at once, or keep in the refrigerator for up to 3 days.

Devil's food **cake**

 CUTS INTO 12 SLICES

Ingredients

12 tbsp soft butter or margarine, plus extra for greasing

3oz (90g) dark chocolate, broken into pieces

¾ cup hot water

1⅓ cups light brown sugar

3 large eggs, beaten

2½ cups all-purpose flour

1½ tsp baking soda

1½ tsp baking powder

1 tsp vanilla extract

⅔ cup sour cream

FROSTING

1½ cups granulated sugar

2 large egg whites

¼ cup hot water

pinch of cream of tartar

SPECIAL EQUIPMENT

3 x 8in (20cm) sandwich cake pans

Method

1 Preheat the oven to 375°F (190°C). Grease the cake pans with butter and line the bottoms with parchment paper.

2 Put the chocolate in a pan with the water. Heat gently, stirring, until the chocolate melts. Cool.

3 Combine the butter and sugar in a bowl and beat until light and fluffy. Gradually add the eggs, beating well.

4 Stir in the melted chocolate. Sift together the flour, baking soda, and baking powder. Fold into the chocolate mixture until evenly blended, then fold in the vanilla extract and sour cream.

5 Divide the mixture evenly among the prepared pans. Bake for about 25 minutes until well-risen, springy to the touch, and just shrinking away from the sides of the pans.

6 Turn the cakes onto a wire rack, peel off the lining paper, and let cool.

7 Make the frosting: combine all the ingredients in a heatproof bowl. Set the bowl over a pan of hot water and beat with a hand-held mixer for 12 minutes or until the mixture is white, thick, and stands in peaks.

8 Use half of the frosting to sandwich the layers together, then spread the remainder over the top and side of the cake, swirling it decoratively and pulling it into peaks with the flat of a small palette knife.

Chocolate & orange mousse cake

 CUTS INTO 12 SLICES

Ingredients

CAKE

butter for greasing

4 large eggs

½ cup granulated sugar

½ cup self-rising flour

⅓ cup cocoa powder

MOUSSE

6oz (175g) dark chocolate, broken into pieces

grated zest and juice of 1 orange

1 tsp powdered gelatin

2 large eggs, separated

1¼ cups heavy cream, whipped until thick

DECORATION

1¼ cups heavy or whipping cream, whipped until thick

strips of orange zest, blanched

SPECIAL EQUIPMENT

deep 9in (23cm) springform cake pan

Method

1 Preheat the oven to 350°F (180°C). Lightly butter the pan and line the bottom with parchment paper. Whisk the eggs with the sugar until the mixture is light and pale. Gently fold in the flour and cocoa powder and turn the mixture into the prepared pan.

2 Bake the cake for 40–45 minutes until the cake is well-risen and beginning to shrink away from the sides of the pan. Turn onto a wire rack, peel off the lining paper, and let cool.

3 Cut the cake in half horizontally. Put one half back into the pan.

4 Make the mousse: put the chocolate into a heatproof bowl set over a pan of hot water. Heat gently, stirring occasionally, until the chocolate has melted. Let cool slightly.

5 Strain the orange juice into a small heatproof bowl and sprinkle in the gelatin. Leave for 3 minutes or until spongy, then stand the bowl in a saucepan of gently simmering water for 3 minutes or until the gelatin has dissolved.

6 Stir the egg yolks and orange zest into the cooled chocolate. Slowly stir in the dissolved gelatin, then fold in the whipped cream. In a separate bowl, whisk the egg whites until stiff but not dry, then gently fold into the chocolate mixture until well-blended.

7 Pour the mousse on top of the cake layer in the pan. Put the remaining cake layer on top. Cover and chill in the refrigerator until the mousse filling is set.

8 Remove the side of the pan and slide the cake onto a serving plate. Decorate with cream and orange zest.

Passing through a village in Devon, England, I stopped at a tea shop and had a piece of wonderful carrot cake. The owner kindly gave me the recipe and it's loved by one and all.

Pineapple & carrot **cake**

 CUTS INTO 8 SLICES

Ingredients

¾ cup sunflower oil, plus extra for greasing

1½ cups self-rising flour

1¼ cups granulated sugar

1½ tsp ground cinnamon

2 large eggs, lightly beaten

1 tsp vanilla extract

1 large carrot, grated

1 cup chopped walnuts

¾ cups shredded coconut

1 x 7oz (220g) can pineapple slices, drained, chopped, and dried thoroughly

FROSTING

7oz (200g) full-fat cream cheese

7 tbsp butter, softened

2 cups confectioners' sugar

1 tsp vanilla extract

SPECIAL EQUIPMENT

2 x 8in (20cm) cake pans

Method

1 Preheat the oven to 350°F (180°C). Grease the pans and line the bottoms with parchment paper. Put the flour into a large mixing bowl, add the sugar and cinnamon, and stir together.

2 Add the oil, eggs, and vanilla extract and beat well with a wooden spoon or spatula. Fold in the carrot, walnuts, coconut, and pineapple and beat until smooth.

3 Spoon evenly into the cake pans and bake for 35 minutes or until well-risen and golden brown. To check that the cakes are cooked in the middle, insert a skewer into the center—if it comes out clean, they are done. Transfer to a wire rack and let cool.

4 To make the frosting, put the cream cheese and butter into a bowl, sift in the confectioners' sugar, add the vanilla extract, and beat with a hand-held mixer until smooth.

5 Remove the cakes from the pans and peel off the parchment paper. Turn one cake upside down onto a serving plate and spread with half the frosting. Set the other cake on top and spread the remaining frosting over the top.

This is now a traditional British Easter cake, but originally it was given by girls to their mothers on Mother's Day.

Simnel cake

 CUTS INTO 12 SLICES

Ingredients

12 tbsp soft butter or margarine, plus extra for greasing

1 cup light brown sugar

3 large eggs

1¼ cups self-rising flour

1 cup golden raisins

½ cup currants

½ cup glacé cherries, quartered, rinsed, and dried

¼ cup candied peel, roughly chopped

grated zest of 1 large lemon

1 tsp pumpkin pie spice

FILLING AND DECORATION

1lb (500g) almond paste

2 tbsp apricot jam

1 large egg white

SPECIAL EQUIPMENT

deep 8in (20cm) round loose-bottomed cake pan

Method

1 Roll out one-third of the almond paste. Using the base of the cake pan as a guide, cut out an 8in (20cm) round.

2 Preheat the oven to 300°F (150°C). Grease the cake pan and line the bottom and sides with parchment paper.

3 Combine all the cake ingredients in a bowl. Beat well until thoroughly blended. Spoon half of the cake mixture into the prepared pan and smooth the surface. Top with the round of almond paste.

4 Spoon the remaining cake mixture on top and level the surface. Bake for 1¾ hours or until golden brown and firm to the touch.

5 Cover the top of the cake with parchment paper if it is browning too quickly. Let cool for 10 minutes, then remove from the pan and let cool completely.

6 Warm the jam and use to brush the top of the cake.

7 To decorate the cake, roll out half of the remaining almond paste and use the pan to cut out an 8in (20cm) round. Put on top of the jam and crimp the edges. Roll the remaining almond paste into 11 even-sized balls. Place around the edge of the cake, attaching them with egg white.

8 Brush the tops of the balls and the almond paste with egg white. Place under a hot broiler for 1–2 minutes, until the balls are golden.

Marbled coffee ring cake

 CUTS INTO 12 SLICES

Ingredients

17 tbsp butter, softened, plus extra for greasing

1 cup granulated sugar

4 large eggs

1½ cups self-rising flour

2 tsp instant coffee

1 tbsp hot water

1oz (30g) white chocolate

ICING

4 tbsp butter, softened

3 tbsp milk

2 tbsp instant coffee

1⅔ cups confectioners' sugar, sifted

SPECIAL EQUIPMENT

8-cup capacity ring mold or 9in (23cm) tube pan

Method

1 Preheat the oven to 350°F (180°C). Lightly grease the ring mold with butter.

2 Combine the butter, sugar, eggs, and flour in a large bowl. Beat until smooth.

3 Put half of the mixture into another bowl. Dissolve the instant coffee in the measured hot water and stir into one-half of the cake mixture.

4 Drop tablespoonfuls of the plain mixture into the ring mold, then tablespoonfuls of the coffee mixture on top of the plain mixture. Marble by swirling together with a skewer.

5 Bake for 40 minutes or until well-risen and firm to the touch. Let cool for a few minutes, then turn onto a wire rack set over a baking sheet and cool completely.

6 Make the icing: combine the butter, milk, and coffee in a pan and heat, stirring, until smooth. Remove from the heat and beat in the confectioners' sugar until smooth and glossy.

7 Let cool, then pour over the cake, spreading it over the sides to cover completely. Let set.

8 Melt the white chocolate in a heatproof bowl over a pan of hot water. Cool slightly, then spoon into a plastic bag. Snip off a corner of the bag and drizzle the chocolate over the cake. Let set.

Battenburg cake

 CUTS INTO 12 SLICES

Ingredients

9 tbsp soft butter or margarine, plus extra for greasing

½ cup granulated sugar

2 extra large eggs

⅓ cup rice flour

1 cup self-rising flour

a few drops of vanilla extract

1½ tsp cocoa powder

3 tbsp apricot jam

8oz (250g) almond paste

SPECIAL EQUIPMENT

shallow 8in (20cm) square cake pan

Method

1 Preheat the oven to 325°F (160°C). Lightly grease the cake pan with butter. Line the bottom of the pan with parchment paper.

2 Beat the butter, sugar, eggs, rice flour, flour, and vanilla extract in a large bowl for 2 minutes or until the mixture is smooth and evenly combined.

3 Spoon half of the mixture into one half of the prepared pan. Dissolve the cocoa in a little hot water to make a thick paste and add to the remaining cake mixture in the bowl. Mix well, then spoon into the other half of the pan.

4 Bake the mixture for 35 minutes or until the cake is well-risen and springy to the touch. Turn onto a wire rack, peel off the lining paper, and cool.

5 Trim the edges of the cake. Cut it into 4 equal strips down the length of the 2 colors.

6 Warm the apricot jam in a small saucepan. Stack the cake strips, alternating the colors to give a checkerboard effect and sticking them together with the apricot jam.

7 Roll out the almond paste into an oblong that is the same length as the cake and wide enough to wrap around it. Put the cake on top, then brush with jam. Wrap the almond paste around the cake, pressing it on gently and making the seam in 1 corner. Turn to hide the seam.

8 Score the top with a crisscross pattern and crimp the edges with your fingertips to make a decorative effect.

Pineapple **upside-down cake**

 CUTS INTO 8 SLICES

Ingredients

4 tbsp butter, softened, plus extra for greasing

⅓ cup light brown sugar

1 x 7oz (225g) can pineapple rings in natural juice, drained, and juice reserved

4 dried apricots, coarsely chopped

CAKE

9 tbsp butter, softened

½ cup granulated sugar

2 large eggs, beaten

1½ cups self-rising flour

SPECIAL EQUIPMENT

7in (18cm) round cake pan

Method

1 Preheat the oven to 350°F (180°C). Lightly butter the pan and line the bottom with parchment paper. Cream together the butter and sugar and spread evenly over the parchment paper.

2 Arrange the pineapple rings on top of the butter and sugar mixture, and sprinkle the chopped dried apricots among the pineapple rings.

3 Make the cake: put the butter, granulated sugar, eggs, and flour into a large bowl with 2 tbsp of the reserved pineapple juice. Beat for 2 minutes or until smooth and well blended. Spoon the mixture on top of the pineapple rings and level the surface.

4 Bake for about 45 minutes until the cake is well-risen and springy to the touch. Invert the cake onto a warmed serving plate, and serve at once.

Apricot upside-down cake

Substitute 1 x 14oz (400g) can apricot halves for the pineapple, and 2 tbsp chopped candied ginger for the dried apricots.

Swiss **roll**

 CUTS INTO 8 SLICES

Ingredients

butter for greasing

4 large eggs

½ cup granulated sugar, plus extra for sprinkling

1 cup self-rising flour

confectioners' sugar for sprinkling

FILLING

about ¼ cup raspberry jam

SPECIAL EQUIPMENT

9 x 13in (23 x 33cm) Swiss roll pan

Method

1 Preheat the oven to 425°F (220°C). Lightly butter the Swiss roll pan, line with parchment paper, then lightly butter the parchment.

2 Put the eggs and sugar into a large bowl. Whisk together with an electric mixer at high speed until the mixture is pale and thick enough to leave a trail when the beaters are lifted out.

3 Sift the flour into the egg mixture and fold in gently but thoroughly.

4 Turn the mixture into the prepared pan and tilt to spread the mixture evenly, particularly into the corners.

5 Bake for 10 minutes or until the cake is golden and starting to shrink away from the sides of the pan.

6 Invert the cake onto a large piece of parchment paper that has been liberally sprinkled with granulated sugar. Peel off the lining paper and trim the edges of the cake with a sharp knife.

7 Roll up the cake and the parchment paper together, from one of the short ends. Let stand for 2–3 minutes.

8 Unroll the cake and remove the parchment paper. Warm the jam, spread the warm jam on the cake, and roll up again. Wrap tightly in parchment paper and let cool. Unwrap, dust with confectioners' sugar, and serve in slices.

Fairy cakes are always so popular. These are a basic vanilla cake mix with lemon icing. Decorate them with creative flair. I like to use jelly beans, gum drops, and malted milk balls.

Fairy **cakes**

 MAKES 24

Ingredients

10 tbsp butter, softened

⅔ cup granulated sugar

1¼ cups self-rising flour

1½ tsp vanilla extract

3 large eggs

candies of your choice to decorate

FROSTING

1¼ cups confectioners' sugar

about 3 tbsp lemon juice

SPECIAL EQUIPMENT

1 x 24-hole mini muffin pan, greased or lined with paper liners

Method

1 Preheat the oven to 350°F (180°C). Put all the ingredients for the cakes into a large mixing bowl and beat with a hand-held mixer until smooth. Spoon evenly into the pan.

2 Bake for 12–15 minutes or until risen and pale golden brown. Set aside to cool, then remove the cakes from the pan.

3 To make the frosting, sift the confectioners' sugar into a bowl and add enough lemon juice to make a fairly stiff paste. Spoon a circle of the frosting on the top of each cake. While the frosting is still soft, decorate with the candies of your choice.

Chocolate chip fairy cakes

Add scant ¼ cup dark chocolate chips to the basic cake mix.

Orange fairy cakes

Add the grated zest of 1 orange to the basic cake mix. For the frosting, use orange juice or orange blossom water instead of lemon juice.

Rose water fairy cakes

For the frosting, use 2 tbsp rose water and 1 tbsp water instead of the lemon juice.

Chocolate
cupcakes

 MAKES 12

Ingredients

½ cup cocoa powder

about ¼ cup boiling water

¾ cup margarine

3 large eggs

⅔ cup granulated sugar

1 cup self-rising flour

FROSTING

4 tbsp butter

⅓ cup cocoa powder

about 3 tbsp milk

1¾ cups confectioners' sugar

SPECIAL EQUIPMENT

1 x 12-hole muffin pans
and 12 paper liners

Method

1 Preheat the oven to 400°F (200°C) and line the muffin pan with paper liners. Sift the cocoa powder into a large bowl, pour in the boiling water, and mix into a thick paste. Add the remaining cake ingredients and mix with a hand-held mixer (or beat well with a wooden spoon).

2 Divide the mixture equally among the 12 paper liners. Bake for about 12–15 minutes until well-risen and springy to the touch. Cool in the liners on a wire rack.

3 Make the frosting: melt the butter, then pour it into a bowl. Sift in the cocoa powder and stir to mix. Stir in the milk and then sift in the confectioners' sugar a little at a time to make a glossy, spreadable frosting. Spread the frosting over the cakes and let set before serving.

Opposite, clockwise from top left:
Double-chocolate muffins (p26), Best-ever
brownies (p87), Chocolate cupcakes.

Lemon cupcakes with lemon frosting

 MAKES 12

Ingredients

9 tbsp soft butter

1 cup self-rising flour

½ cup granulated sugar

2 tbsp milk

2 extra large eggs

finely grated zest of 1 small lemon

LEMON FROSTING

9 tbsp soft unsalted butter

2¼ cups confectioners' sugar, sifted

juice of 1 small lemon

edible silver balls or glitter to decorate

SPECIAL EQUIPMENT

**deep 12-hole muffin pan
and 12 paper liners**

Method

1 Preheat the oven to 350°F (180°C) and line the muffin pan with the paper liners. Put all the cake ingredients into a bowl and beat with a hand-held mixer until evenly combined and smooth.

2 Divide the mixture among the paper liners. Bake for 20–25 minutes until well-risen and light golden brown. Transfer the cakes in their liners to a wire rack and let cool.

3 Make the frosting: put the butter and half of the confectioners' sugar into a large bowl and beat with a hand-held mixer until evenly combined and smooth. Add the lemon juice and the remaining confectioners' sugar, and beat again until light and fluffy. Spread the frosting over the cold cupcakes and decorate with silver balls or glitter.

Cupcakes are the cake of the moment, with some shops specializing in just them. These are made in muffin pans, which are fairly large, but make them in mini muffin pans if you wish—you should get 18 mini cupcakes.

Coffee & walnut cupcakes

 MAKES 12

Ingredients

1 tbsp instant coffee granules

1 tbsp boiling water

8 tbsp butter, softened

1¼ cups self-rising flour

⅔ cup granulated sugar

2 tbsp milk

2 extra large eggs

¼ cup walnuts, chopped

COFFEE FROSTING

2 tsp instant coffee granules

2 tsp boiling water

7 tbsp butter, at room temperature

1¾ cups confectioners' sugar

12 walnut halves to decorate

SPECIAL EQUIPMENT

12-hole muffin pan lined with 12 paper muffin liners

Method

1 Preheat the oven to 350°F (180°C). Put the coffee granules and water into a large mixing bowl and stir until smooth. Add the butter, flour, sugar, milk, and eggs and mix with a hand-held mixer until smooth. Stir in the walnuts, then spoon into the muffin liners.

2 Bake in the center of the oven for 20–25 minutes or until risen and golden brown. Transfer to a wire rack and cool completely.

3 Make the frosting: put the coffee granules and boiling water into a large bowl and stir until smooth. Add the butter, sift in the confectioners' sugar, and stir until smooth and free of streaks.

4 Spoon on to the cupcakes, then decorate each one with a walnut half.

🔍 Cook's know-how

SOFTENING BUTTER

To make sure the butter is soft enough to work with, cut it into small cubes and pop into a bowl of lukewarm water. After 10 minutes or so, squeeze one of the cubes—it should be nice and soft. You can then drain the cubes and use them.

Arranged on a tiered cakestand, a dozen cupcakes (see page 56) make a spectacular centerpiece for any party. I like to bake them in silver or floral muffin liners. Serve one per person.

Cupcake tier

 MAKES 12

Ingredients

GLACÉ FROSTING

juice of 1 lemon

2 cups confectioners' sugar

CHOCOLATE CURLS

bar of white chocolate, at room temperature

bar of chocolate, at room temperature

Method

1 Make a dozen cupcakes, following the recipe on page 56. You won't need the coffee frosting and walnuts.

2 To make the glacé frosting, warm the lemon juice in a pan. Put the confectioners' sugar into a mixing bowl and gradually add enough lemon juice to make a smooth, glossy frosting. Spoon the frosting onto the cupcakes and let set.

3 Meanwhile, shave curls from the chocolate bars with a vegetable peeler.

4 Once the frosting has set, decorate the cupcakes with a mixture of white chocolate curls and chocolate curls.

🔍 Cook's know-how

DECORATING CUPCAKES

When it comes to decorating cupcakes, let your imagination run riot. But keep the tier looking elegant and classy, not chaotic. Crystallized flowers look pretty, as do silver balls or silver hearts. Or decorate the edges of the cakestand with fresh flowers. The beauty of the cupcake tier is that you can match the decorations to suit the occasion. For a child's birthday party, for instance, you could decorate one of the cupcakes with a candle. Tiny colored candies such as jelly beans and Smarties also work well.

Baklava

 MAKES 20 SQUARES

Ingredients

2⅓ cups walnut pieces, finely chopped

⅓ cup light brown sugar

1 tsp ground cinnamon

12 tbsp butter, melted,
plus extra for greasing

24 sheets of filo dough, weighing
about 1lb (500g)

⅓ cup honey

2 tbsp lemon juice

SPECIAL EQUIPMENT

shallow 7 x 9in (18 x 23cm)
rectangular cake pan

Method

1 Preheat the oven to 425°F (220°C). Mix together the walnuts, sugar, and cinnamon.

2 Lightly butter the cake pan and lay 1 sheet of filo dough in the bottom of the pan, allowing the sheet to come up the sides. (If necessary, cut the sheets in half to fit in the pan.) Brush the sheet with a little melted butter.

3 Repeat with 5 more filo sheets, layering and brushing each one with the butter. Sprinkle with one-third of the nut mixture.

4 Repeat this process twice, using 6 more sheets of filo dough each time, brushing each sheet with butter and sprinkling the nut mixture over every sixth sheet. Finish with 6 buttered sheets of filo dough, and lightly brush the top with melted butter.

5 Trim the edges of the filo, then, using a sharp knife, cut about halfway through the layers to make 20 squares.

6 Bake for 15 minutes, then reduce the oven temperature to 350°F (180°C) and bake for 10–15 minutes until the filo is crisp and golden brown. Remove the baklava from the oven.

7 Heat the honey and lemon juice in a heavy saucepan until the honey has melted. Spoon over the hot baklava. Let cool in the pan for 1–2 hours. Cut into the marked squares, and serve the baklava at room temperature.

Coffee éclairs

 MAKES 10–12

Ingredients

butter for greasing

1 quantity choux pastry (see p13)

1 large egg, beaten

1¼ cups whipping cream, whipped

COFFEE FROSTING

1 tsp instant coffee

3 tbsp butter

2 tbsp water

⅔ cup confectioners' sugar

Method

1 Preheat the oven to 425°F (220°C). Butter a baking sheet and sprinkle with water. Spoon the choux into a piping bag fitted with a ½in (1cm) plain nozzle, pipe into 3in (7cm) lengths, and brush with beaten egg. Bake for 10 minutes, then reduce the temperature to 375°F (190°C) and bake for 20 minutes. Split in half and cool on a rack.

2 Spoon the whipped cream onto the bottom halves of the éclairs.

3 Make the frosting: put the coffee, butter, and water in a bowl over a pan of water. Heat gently until the butter melts. Remove from the heat and beat in the confectioners' sugar. Dip the top half of each éclair in the frosting, then place on top of the cream. Let the frosting cool before serving.

Religieuses

 MAKES 10

Ingredients

butter for greasing

1 quantity choux pastry (see p13)

1 large egg, beaten

1¼ cups whipping cream, whipped

1 quantity warm Wicked Chocolate Frosting (see p64)

Method

1 Preheat the oven to 425°F (220°C). Butter a baking sheet and sprinkle with water. Spoon the choux into a piping bag fitted with a ½in (1cm) plain nozzle, pipe 10 small and 10 slightly larger balls, and brush with beaten egg. Bake for 10 minutes, then reduce the temperature to 375°F (190°C) and bake for 20 minutes. Split one side of each bun and cool on a rack.

2 Reserve about 3 tbsp of the whipped cream. Fill the balls with the remaining whipped cream, spooning it in the sides.

3 Dip the tops of a large and small ball in frosting. Fit a piping bag with a ½in (1cm) star nozzle and pipe the reserved cream on top of the large ball. Gently press the small ball on top of the cream, with the frosting facing up. Repeat with the other balls.

Chocolate profiteroles

 MAKES 12

Ingredients

butter for greasing

1 quantity choux pastry (see p13)

1 large egg, beaten

1¼ cups whipping cream, whipped

WICKED CHOCOLATE FROSTING

5oz (150g) 38% cocoa solids dark chocolate, chopped (or semi-sweet chocolate chips)

⅔ cup heavy cream

Method

1 Preheat the oven to 425°F (220°C). Butter a baking sheet and sprinkle with water. Put 12 tablespoonfuls of choux on the pan and brush with beaten egg. Bake for 10 minutes, then reduce the temperature to 375°F (190°C) and bake for 20 minutes. Split each profiterole in half and cool on a rack.

2 Make the Wicked Chocolate Frosting: gently melt the chocolate with the heavy cream in a bowl over a pan of simmering water, stirring until smooth and shiny (be careful not to let it get too hot).

3 Sandwich the profiteroles together with the whipped cream, place on individual plates, and drizzle with the chocolate frosting.

Opposite, clockwise from top left: Coffee éclairs (p62), Religieuses (p63), Chocolate profiteroles

Cookies, bars & brownies

Viennese fingers

 MAKES 12

Ingredients

12 tbsp butter, plus extra for greasing

⅓ **cup granulated sugar**

1½ **cups self-rising flour**

3oz (90g) dark chocolate, broken into pieces

Method

1 Preheat the oven to 325°F (160°C). Lightly butter 2 baking sheets. Combine the butter and sugar in a bowl and cream together until pale and fluffy. Stir in the flour and beat until well-combined.

2 Spoon the mixture into a piping bag with a medium star nozzle. Pipe into 3in (7cm) lengths on the baking sheets. Bake for about 20 minutes until golden. Cool on a wire rack.

3 Put the chocolate into a heatproof bowl. Set the bowl over a pan of hot water and heat gently until the chocolate has melted. Dip both ends of each cookie into the chocolate. Let set on the wire rack.

Pinwheel cookies

 MAKES 18

Ingredients

VANILLA DOUGH

4 tbsp butter, at room temperature, plus extra for greasing

2½ tbsp granulated sugar

½ cup all-purpose flour

a few drops of vanilla extract

about 1 tbsp water

COFFEE DOUGH

4 tbsp butter, at room temperature

2½ tbsp granulated sugar

½ cup all-purpose flour

1 tbsp coffee extract

milk for brushing

Cook's know-how

If the doughs become too soft and difficult to roll out, put each piece of dough between sheets of parchment paper before rolling.

Method

1 Combine the ingredients for the vanilla dough in a bowl and mix well, adding just enough water to bind. Knead lightly, then wrap and chill for at least 2 hours until very firm.

2 Mix the ingredients for the coffee dough, using the coffee extract to bind. Wrap and chill for at least 2 hours until very firm.

3 On a lightly floured work surface, roll out each dough to a rectangle about 7 x 10in (18 x 25cm).

4 Brush the coffee dough with a little milk, then place the vanilla dough on top. Roll up together like a roulade, starting at a narrow end.

5 Wrap the roll tightly in foil and let chill in the refrigerator for about 30 minutes or until firm. Preheat the oven to 350°F (180°C).

6 Lightly grease 1–2 baking sheets. Cut the dough roll into about 18 thin slices and place them well apart on the baking sheets.

7 Bake for about 20 minutes until the vanilla dough is a very pale golden color.

8 Let the cookies cool on the baking sheets for a few minutes, then transfer to a wire rack and let cool completely.

Fridge cookies

 MAKES 50

Ingredients

1¾ cups all-purpose flour

1 tsp baking powder

9 tbsp butter, plus extra for greasing

⅔ cup granulated sugar

⅔ cup walnuts, finely chopped

1 large egg, beaten

1 tsp vanilla extract

Method

1 Sift the flour and baking powder into a bowl. Rub in the butter with your fingertips until the mixture resembles bread crumbs. Mix in the sugar and walnuts. Add the beaten egg and vanilla extract and stir to form a smooth dough.

2 Shape the dough into a cylinder about 2in (5cm) in diameter. Wrap in foil, roll to give smooth sides, and refrigerate for about 8 hours.

3 Preheat the oven to 375°F (190°C). Lightly butter several baking sheets. Cut the cylinder into thin slices and place the cookies on the baking sheets. Bake for 10–12 minutes until golden.

Everyone loves cookies. And no one will be able to resist this deliciously gooey combination of pecans and chocolate. The cookies keep well in a container for a couple of days.

Pecan & chocolate chip **cookies**

 MAKES 24

Ingredients

7 tbsp butter, at room temperature

¼ cup granulated sugar

1¼ cups self-rising flour, plus extra for dusting

½ tsp vanilla extract

¼ cup milk chocolate chips

⅓ cup pecans, chopped

Method

1 Preheat the oven to 350°F (180°C). Put the butter and sugar into a bowl and mix together with a wooden spoon until light and fluffy. Stir in the flour, then add the vanilla extract, chocolate chips, and pecans and mix to a soft dough.

2 Knead the dough lightly on a floured work surface, then divide into 24 balls. Flatten the balls with the palm of your hand and arrange on two baking sheets lined with parchment paper. Space them out so they have room to spread.

3 Bake for 20–25 minutes or until lightly golden. Transfer to a wire rack to cool.

Gingerbread Christmas cookies

 MAKES 24

Ingredients

⅓ cup blackstrap molasses

¼ cup dark brown sugar

4 tbsp butter, softened

¾ teaspoon baking soda

¼ teaspoon ground allspice

¼ teaspoon ground cinnamon

¼ teaspoon ground cloves

¼ teaspoon ground ginger

1 large egg

about 2⅔ cups all-purpose flour

ornamental Icing (see box, below)

SPECIAL EQUIPMENT

3½in (8cm) festive-shaped cookie cutters

Ornamental icing

In a large bowl, beat 4 cups confectioners' sugar, sifted, 5 tablespoons warm water, and 3 tablespoons albumen powder with an electric mixer. Beat until the mixture is so stiff that when a knife is drawn through the mixture it will leave a clean path.

Method

1 In large bowl, combine the blackstrap molasses, brown sugar, butter, baking soda, allspice, cinnamon, cloves, ginger, egg, and 1 cup of the flour. With an electric mixer, beat the ingredients for 2 minutes, frequently scraping the bowl with a rubber spatula. With a wooden spoon, stir in enough of the remaining flour to make a stiff dough. Shape the dough into ball; wrap. Use the dough immediately or refrigerate to use within 2 days.

2 Preheat oven to 350°F (180°C). On a lightly floured surface, with a floured rolling pin, roll out half of the dough ⅛in (3mm) thick.

3 Cut out as many cookies as possible. With a spatula, place the cookies about ½in (1cm) apart on a large baking sheet.

4 Bake the cookies for 12 minutes or until the edges are firm. With a spatula, immediately loosen the cookies from the pan and transfer to wire racks to cool. Repeat with remaining dough and trimmings.

5 If not decorating the cookies immediately, wrap in freezer paper or foil, seal, label, and freeze. Before decorating, unwrap the frozen cookies and thaw for 1 hour.

6 Prepare the ornamental icing: spoon the icing into a piping bag with a small writing tube, or use a paper piping bag with the tip cut to make a ⅛in (3mm) hole; pipe decorative outlines and designs on each cookie. Set the cookies aside to let the icing dry completely, about 1 hour.

Almond **tuiles**

 MAKES 30

Ingredients

2 large egg whites

½ **cup granulated sugar**

½ **cup all-purpose flour**

½ **tsp vanilla extract**

4 tbsp butter, melted and cooled, plus extra for greasing

¼ **cup sliced almonds**

Method

1 Preheat the oven to 350°F (180°C). Line a baking sheet with parchment paper. Put the egg whites into a bowl and beat in the sugar until frothy. Stir in the flour and vanilla extract, then add the melted butter.

2 Put 6 teaspoonfuls of the mixture onto the baking sheet, spacing them well apart to allow for spreading. Flatten each with a fork.

3 Sprinkle with the almonds. Bake for about 6 minutes until golden brown around the edges but still pale in the middle.

4 Let the cookies cool on the baking sheet for a few seconds, then lift off with a spatula and gently lay them over a greased rolling pin to give the traditional curved shape.

5 Allow the cookies to set, then lift off onto a wire rack and let cool.

6 Cook and shape the remaining mixture in batches, cooking one batch while another is setting on the rolling pin.

Ginger **snaps**

 MAKES 15

Ingredients

4 tbsp butter, plus extra for greasing

¼ cup golden syrup or 2 tbsp corn syrup plus 2 tbsp honey

1 cup self-rising flour

2 tsp ground ginger

1 tsp ground cinnamon

½ tsp baking soda

1 tbsp granulated sugar

Method

1 Lightly grease 2 baking sheets with butter. Combine the butter and syrup in a small saucepan and heat gently until melted. Let the mixture cool slightly. Preheat the oven to 375°F (190°C).

2 Sift the flour, spices, and baking soda into a bowl and stir in the sugar. Add the cooled syrup mixture and stir to mix to a soft but not sticky dough.

3 Roll the dough into balls about the size of walnuts and place well apart on the baking sheets. Flatten the dough balls slightly with the heel of your hand.

4 Bake for about 15 minutes. Let the cookies cool on the baking sheets for a few minutes, then transfer to a wire rack and let cool completely.

Brandy **snaps**

 MAKES 15

Ingredients

6 tbsp butter, plus extra for greasing

½ cup dark brown sugar

¼ cup golden syrup or 2 tbsp corn syrup plus 2 tbsp honey

¾ cup all-purpose flour

¾ tsp ground ginger

¾ tsp lemon juice

Method

1 Preheat the oven to 325°F (160°C). Line a baking sheet with parchment paper. Combine the butter, sugar, and syrup in a saucepan and heat gently until the ingredients have melted and dissolved. Cool slightly, then sift in the flour and ginger. Add the lemon juice and stir well.

2 Place 3–4 teaspoonfuls of the mixture on the baking sheet, leaving plenty of room for the cookies to spread out.

3 Bake for about 8 minutes until the mixture spreads out to form large, thin, dark golden rounds. While the cookies are baking, oil the handles of 4 wooden spoons.

4 Remove the cookies from the oven and leave for 1–2 minutes to firm slightly.

5 Lift a cookie from the paper using a spatula or palette knife, turn the cookie over so that the rough side is on the outside, and wrap around an oiled wooden spoon handle. Repeat with the remaining cookies. Transfer to a wire rack and cool until firm, then slide them off the spoon handles.

6 Continue baking, shaping, and cooling the remaining mixture in batches.

Shortbread

 MAKES 8 WEDGES

Ingredients

1 cup all-purpose flour

½ cup semolina or cornstarch

9 tbsp butter, plus extra for greasing

⅓ cup granulated sugar, plus extra for sprinkling

Method

1 Preheat the oven to 325°F (160°C). Mix the flour with the semolina or cornstarch in a bowl. Add the butter and rub in with your fingertips. Stir in the sugar. Knead the mixture lightly until it forms a smooth dough.

2 Lightly butter a baking sheet. Roll out the dough on a lightly floured work surface into a 7in (18cm) round. Lift onto the baking sheet. Crimp the edges to decorate, prick all over with a fork, and mark into 8 wedges with a sharp knife. Chill until firm.

3 Bake for 35 minutes or until a pale golden brown color. Mark the wedges again and sprinkle the shortbread with sugar.

4 Let the shortbread cool on the baking sheet for about 5 minutes, then lift off carefully with a palette knife and transfer to a wire rack to cool completely. Cut into wedges to serve.

Pink almond macaroons

 MAKES 40

Ingredients

2 cups confectioners' sugar, sifted

2 cups ground almonds

¾ cup granulated sugar

¼ cup cold water

4 extra large egg whites

1 tsp almond extract

red food coloring

FILLING

6 tbsp soft butter

1¼ cups confectioners' sugar, sifted

raspberry jam

SPECIAL EQUIPMENT

piping bag with ½in (1cm) plain nozzle

Method

1 Line 2 baking sheets with parchment paper. Combine the confectioners' sugar and almonds in a bowl and set aside.

2 Put the granulated sugar and water into a stainless steel pan. Heat gently over low heat, stirring, until the sugar has dissolved. Bring to a boil and boil for a few minutes without stirring, until you have a shiny, clear syrup, the consistency of half-and-half. If you have a sugar thermometer it should read 230°F (110°C), no more. Remove from the heat and let cool slightly.

3 Put 2 of the egg whites into a bowl and beat with a hand-held mixer on high speed until stiff but not dry. Slowly pour in the sugar syrup in a thin, steady stream, beating constantly until all the syrup is used and you have a shiny meringue. Add the remaining 2 unbeaten egg whites to the sugar and almonds and mix to a very thick paste with a wooden spoon. Add the almond extract and stir in just enough food coloring to make the mixture pink. Add a heaping tablespoonful of the meringue, beat well, then carefully fold in the remaining meringue until the mixture is an even pink color. Do not overmix or it will be too runny.

4 Fill the piping bag with the mixture. Pipe 40 small rounds, each about 1½in (3.5cm) in diameter, onto each baking sheet. If you do not have a piping bag, use 2 teaspoons to spoon the mixture onto the pans. Set aside to dry for about an hour until a skin forms on top. Preheat the oven to 300°F (150°C).

5 Bake for about 25 minutes until firm and glossy on top. Turn the oven off and let the macaroons cool in the oven for about an hour. Transfer to a wire rack with a damp palette knife and let cool completely.

6 Cream the butter and half of the confectioners' sugar in a bowl, beating until pale and fluffy. Beat in the remaining sugar a little at a time until the mixture is smooth. Spread a little jam and buttercream over the bottom of 40 macaroons, then sandwich together with the remaining macaroons.

Coconut macaroons

 MAKES 26

Ingredients

3 large egg whites

1½ cups confectioners' sugar

½ cup ground almonds

a few drops of almond extract

3 cups shredded coconut

about 13 whole almonds, blanched and halved

Method

1 Preheat the oven to 300°F (150°C). Line 2 baking sheets with parchment paper.

2 Whisk the egg whites thoroughly until stiff but not dry. Sift in the confectioners' sugar and fold it in gently. Fold in the ground almonds, almond extract, and shredded coconut.

3 Put teaspoonfuls of the coconut mixture onto the baking sheets. Top each with an almond half.

4 Bake for about 25 minutes until golden brown and crisp on the outside and soft in the middle.

5 Let the macaroons cool on a wire rack. These are best served on the day of making.

Chocolate whoopie pies

 MAKES 15

Ingredients

3 cups all-purpose flour

¾ cup cocoa powder

½ tsp baking soda

10 tbsp soft butter

1 cup light brown sugar

1 large egg

1¼ cups sour cream

FILLING

9 tbsp soft butter

2 cups confectioners' sugar, sifted

1 tsp vanilla extract

TOPPING

¾ cup confectioners' sugar

2 tbsp cocoa powder

2½ tbsp cold water

colored sprinkles to decorate

Method

1 Preheat the oven to 350°F (180°C). Line 2 baking sheets with parchment paper. Sift the flour, cocoa powder, and baking soda into a bowl.

2 Put the butter, sugar, egg, and sour cream into another bowl, and beat with a hand-held mixer until evenly combined and smooth. Add half of the flour mixture and beat until smooth again, then add the remaining flour mixture and beat until the mixture is very thick and smooth.

3 Divide the mixture in half and put 15 rounded spoonfuls on each baking sheet, leaving room between them for the cakes to spread during baking.

4 Bake for 15–20 minutes until risen and firm to the touch—they will be cracked a little in the middle. Let cool slightly, then transfer to a wire rack and let cool completely.

5 Make the filling: put the butter into a bowl with half of the confectioners' sugar and beat with a hand-held mixer until smooth and creamy. Add the remaining sugar and beat again, then stir in the vanilla extract.

6 Make the topping: sift the confectioners' sugar and cocoa powder into a bowl. Add the water and mix to a smooth, spreadable icing. Sandwich the pies together with the filling, spread the icing on top, and scatter with colored sprinkles.

Iced lime bars

 MAKES 12 SQUARES

Ingredients

12 tbsp soft butter or margarine, plus extra for greasing

²⁄₃ **cup granulated sugar**

1¾ **cups self-rising flour**

1½ **tsp baking powder**

3 large eggs

3 tbsp milk

finely grated zest of 2 limes, plus extra for decoration

ICING

1¾ **cups confectioners' sugar**

juice of 2 limes

SPECIAL EQUIPMENT

9 x 13in (23 x 33cm) cake pan

Method

1 Preheat the oven to 350°F (180°C). Lightly grease the pan and line the bottom with parchment paper.

2 Combine all the cake ingredients in a large bowl and beat well for about 2 minutes or until smooth and thoroughly blended.

3 Pour into the prepared pan and level the surface. Bake for 35–40 minutes until the cake is well-risen, springy to the touch, and beginning to shrink away from the sides of the cake pan.

4 Let cool slightly in the pan, then turn onto a wire rack, peel off the lining paper, and cool.

5 Make the icing: sift the confectioners' sugar into a bowl. Mix in enough of the lime juice to give a runny consistency. Pour over the cooled cake, spreading carefully with a palette knife, and let set. When cold, cut into squares, and serve with a little lime zest grated over the top.

Chocolate and mint bars

Mix ¼ cup cocoa powder with ¼ cup hot water and let cool. Add to the basic cake ingredients with ¼ cup chopped fresh mint. For the icing, break 8oz (225g) chocolate into pieces and put into a heatproof bowl with 6 tbsp butter and ¼ cup hot water. Put the bowl over a saucepan of hot water and heat gently until the chocolate has melted. Beat together until smooth and shiny, then spread over the top of the cooled cake.

Lemon bars are always a big hit and I think this variation with orange is particularly delicious. It's also very easy to make.

Iced orange & lemon **bars**

 MAKES 12 SQUARES

Ingredients

16 tbsp butter, at room temperature

1 cup granulated sugar

2½ cups self-rising flour

4 large eggs

¼ cup milk

grated zest of ½ lemon

grated zest of ½ small orange

ICING

1¾ cups confectioners' sugar

1 tbsp lemon juice

2 tbsp orange juice

grated zest of ½ lemon

grated zest of ½ small orange

SPECIAL EQUIPMENT

9 x 12in (23 x 30cm) baking pan, lined with foil and greased

Method

1 Preheat the oven to 350°F (180°C). Put the butter, sugar, flour, eggs, and milk into a bowl and mix with a wooden spoon or hand-held mixer until smooth. Stir in the lemon zest and orange zest and pour into the baking pan. Level the top.

2 Bake for 30 minutes or until shrinking away from the sides of the pan and springy to the touch. Let cool in the pan.

3 Make the icing: sift the confectioners' sugar into a bowl, mix in the lemon juice and orange juice, and beat until smooth. Spread evenly over the cold cake, then sprinkle with the lemon zest and orange zest and let set. To serve, cut into 12 squares.

Best-ever brownies

 MAKES 24

Ingredients

16 tbsp margarine, plus extra for greasing

12oz (375g) dark chocolate, broken into pieces

2 tsp instant coffee

2 tbsp hot water

2 large eggs

1 cup granulated sugar

1 tsp vanilla extract

½ cup self-rising flour

1½ cups walnut pieces

1 cup chocolate chips

Cook's know-how

For brownies to be good, they must not be overcooked. The secret is to take them out of the oven just before you think they are done—the middle should be soft and squishy, not set firm. Do not worry if there is a dip in the middle and a crack on the top; this is how it should be, and you will find that the mixture firms up on cooling.

Method

1 Preheat the oven to 375°F (190°C). Grease a 12 x 9in (30 x 23cm) baking pan, line the base with parchment paper, and grease the paper.

2 Put the chocolate and margarine in a bowl and set the bowl on top of a small saucepan of gently simmering water. Melt the chocolate slowly, then remove the bowl from the pan and let the chocolate cool.

3 Put the coffee in another bowl, pour in the hot water, and stir to dissolve. Add the eggs, sugar, and vanilla extract. Gradually beat in the chocolate mixture. Fold in the flour and walnuts, then the chocolate chips.

4 Pour the mixture into the prepared pan and bake for about 40–45 minutes or until firm to the touch. Don't overcook—the crust should be dull and crisp, but the middle should still be gooey. Let cool in the pan, then cut into 24 pieces.

Gingerbread

 MAKES 15 SQUARES

Ingredients

16 tbsp butter or margarine, plus extra for greasing

1 cup dark brown sugar

1 cup blackstrap molasses

3 cups all-purpose flour

5 tsp ground ginger

2 tsp ground cinnamon

2 large eggs, beaten

3 pieces of candied ginger, coarsely chopped

1¼ cups milk

2 tsp baking soda

SPECIAL EQUIPMENT

9 x 13in (23 x 33cm) cake pan

Method

1 Preheat the oven to 325°F (160°C). Lightly grease the pan and line the bottom with parchment paper.

2 Heat the butter, sugar, and molasses in a pan, stirring, until smooth. Cool slightly.

3 Sift in the flour and ground spices. Stir well, then beat in the eggs and candied ginger.

4 Warm the milk in a small, heavy saucepan and add the baking soda. Pour into the gingerbread mixture and stir gently until thoroughly blended.

5 Pour the mixture into the prepared pan. Bake for about 1 hour until well-risen and springy to the touch.

6 Let cool in the pan for a few minutes, then turn onto a wire rack and peel off the paper. Let cool completely, then store in an airtight container for 2–3 days (it improves with keeping). Cut into squares to serve.

Pies, tarts & cobblers

This is a rich dessert, ideal for a Christmas dinner party or lunch. For an everyday dessert, you could use less mincemeat and add some stewed apples, which will give a lighter texture and flavor.

Mincemeat & almond **tart**

 SERVES 10

Ingredients

DOUGH

2 cups all-purpose flour

9 tbsp chilled butter, cut into cubes

¼ cup granulated sugar

1 large egg, beaten

1–2 tbsp water

FILLING

12 tbsp butter, softened

⅔ cup granulated sugar

4 large eggs

1½ cups ground almonds

1 tsp almond extract

about ½ cup good-quality mincemeat

TOPPING

1½ cups confectioners' sugar, sifted

juice of ½ lemon

1–2 tbsp water

½ cup sliced almonds

SPECIAL EQUIPMENT

deep 11in (28cm) loose-bottomed fluted tart pan

Method

1 Make the dough: put the flour into a large bowl. Add the butter and rub in with your fingertips until the mixture resembles fine bread crumbs. Stir in the sugar, then mix in the egg and water to bind to a soft, pliable dough. Wrap the dough in plastic wrap and chill for about 30 minutes.

2 Preheat the oven to 375°F (190°C). Roll out the dough on a lightly floured surface and use to line the pan. Prick the bottom with a fork. Cover and chill while preparing the filling.

3 Make the filling: put the butter and sugar into a large bowl and cream together until pale and fluffy. Add the eggs one at a time, beating well after each addition, then mix in the ground almonds and almond extract.

4 Spread the mincemeat evenly over the bottom of the crust. Pour the almond mixture over the mincemeat.

5 Bake for about 40 minutes until the filling is golden and firm to the touch. Cover loosely with foil if it is browning too much.

6 Meanwhile, make the topping: stir together the confectioners' sugar, lemon juice, and enough water to make a thin glacé icing. Spread evenly over the tart, then sprinkle with the almonds.

7 Return to the oven for 5 minutes or until the icing is shiny and the almonds are lightly colored. Serve warm or cold.

Strawberry & rhubarb **pie**

 SERVES 6–8

Ingredients

DOUGH

1⅓ cups all-purpose flour

6 tbsp chilled butter, cut into cubes

about 2 tbsp cold water

⅔ cup granulated sugar,
plus extra for sprinkling

FILLING

⅓ cup cornstarch

1½lb (750g) rhubarb, cut into ½in
(1cm) slices

1 cinnamon stick, halved

12oz (375g) strawberries,
hulled and halved

SPECIAL EQUIPMENT

9in (23cm) pie dish

Method

1 Make the shortcrust pastry: put the flour into a large bowl, add the butter, and rub in with your fingertips until the mixture resembles fine bread crumbs. Add enough water to bind to a soft but not sticky dough. Wrap the dough in plastic wrap and let chill in the refrigerator for about 30 minutes.

2 Meanwhile, combine the sugar with the cornstarch and toss with the rhubarb, cinnamon, and strawberries. Let soak for 15–20 minutes.

3 Preheat the oven to 425°F (225°C). On a lightly floured surface, divide the dough in half and roll out one half into a thin round to line the bottom and sides of the pie dish.

4 Put the soaked fruit into the pie crust, removing the cinnamon.

5 Roll out the second half of the dough to the same size as the first round. Cut a ½in (1cm) strip from around the edge of the dough.

6 Cut the remaining dough into ½in (1cm) strips and arrange in a lattice on top of the pie. Brush the ends with water and attach the long strip around the rim of the pie. Sprinkle with 1–2 tbsp sugar.

7 Bake for 10 minutes; reduce the oven temperature to 350°F (180°C), and bake for another 30–40 minutes until the fruit is just cooked and the crust golden. Serve warm or cold.

Royal raspberry **tart**

 SERVES 8–10

Ingredients

DOUGH

1⅓ cups all-purpose flour

6 tbsp chilled butter, cut into cubes

about 2 tbsp cold water

FILLING

⅓ cup granulated sugar

2½ tbsp cornstarch

1 tbsp powdered gelatin

2 large eggs plus 1 large egg yolk

1½ cups milk

1 tsp vanilla extract

⅔ cup heavy or whipping cream

1lb (450g) raspberries

SPECIAL EQUIPMENT

10in (25cm) loose-bottomed fluted tart pan

Method

1 Make the dough: put the flour into a large bowl, add the butter, and rub in with your fingertips until the mixture resembles fine bread crumbs. Mix in enough water to make a soft, pliable dough. Wrap the dough in plastic wrap and let chill in the refrigerator for about 30 minutes.

2 In a medium saucepan, combine the sugar, cornstarch, and gelatin. In a medium bowl, with a wire whisk or fork, beat the eggs and egg yolk with milk and vanilla extract until well-mixed; stir into the gelatin mixture. Let stand for 5 minutes to soften the gelatin slightly.

3 Cook over low heat, stirring constantly, until the mixture thickens and coats a spoon well, about 20 minutes. Remove the saucepan from the heat.

4 Pour the custard into a large bowl; cool, then cover and refrigerate until the mixture mounds slightly when dropped from a spoon, about 1 hour, stirring occasionally.

5 Roll out the dough on a lightly floured surface and use to line the tart pan. Chill again for 30 minutes. Preheat the oven to 400°F (200°C). Prick the base and bake for 10 minutes; reduce the oven temperature to 350°F (180°C) and bake for another 30 minutes or until the crust is golden.

6 In a small bowl, whip the heavy or whipping cream until stiff peaks form. With a rubber spatula or wire whisk, fold the whipped cream into the custard.

7 Carefully remove the tart from the pan; place on a serving plate. Spoon the custard into the tart crust and top with the raspberries.

8 Refrigerate the tart for 1 hour or until the custard is completely set.

For a successful double-crust pie, the dough underneath should be properly cooked and not soggy. Putting the dish on a hot baking sheet at the start of baking is the key.

Double-crust apple pie

 SERVES 6

Ingredients

1lb (500g) tart apples, quartered, cored, peeled, and sliced

8oz (250g) sweet apples, quartered, cored, peeled, and sliced

about 2 tbsp granulated sugar, plus extra for sprinkling

2 tbsp water

rough puff pastry (page 12)

milk for glazing

SPECIAL EQUIPMENT

9½in (24cm) pie dish

St. Clement's apple pie

When cooking the apples, add the grated zest and juice of 1 large lemon and 3 tbsp fine-cut orange marmalade to the apples.

Method

1 Put a baking sheet in the oven and preheat the oven to 425°F (220°C). Put the apples into a large pan and add the sugar and water. Cover and cook gently, stirring, for about 10 minutes until the apples are soft and fluffy. Taste for sweetness and add more sugar if necessary. Transfer to a bowl and let the apples cool.

2 Divide the pastry into 2 portions, 1 portion slightly larger than the other. Roll out the larger portion on a lightly floured surface and use to line the pie dish.

3 Spoon the apple filling onto the pie crust, spreading it almost to the edge and then doming it in the middle.

4 Roll out the remaining dough. Brush the edge of the pie crust with a little water, then lay the pastry lid over the apple filling. Trim the edge, then crimp to seal. Make a small hole in the pastry lid to allow the steam to escape.

5 Use the pastry trimmings to make leaves to decorate the pie, attaching them with milk. Brush the pastry lid with milk and sprinkle with sugar.

6 Put the pie dish on the hot baking sheet (this helps ensure a crisp pie crust) and bake for 25–30 minutes until the crust is golden. I love to serve this pie warm with pouring custard (see p150) or vanilla ice cream.

Tarte Tatin

 SERVES 6

Ingredients

DOUGH

1⅓ cups all-purpose flour

9 tbsp chilled butter, cut into cubes

¼ cup confectioners' sugar

1 large egg yolk

about 1 tbsp cold water

FILLING

6 tbsp butter

½ cup dark brown sugar

2lb (1kg) sweet apples

grated zest and juice of 1 lemon

SPECIAL EQUIPMENT

shallow 9in (23cm) round cake pan

Method

1 Make the dough: put the flour into a large bowl and add the butter. Rub in until the mixture resembles fine bread crumbs. Stir in the confectioners' sugar, then mix in the egg yolk and enough water to make a soft, but not sticky, dough. Wrap and chill for 30 minutes.

2 Put the butter and sugar into a pan and heat very gently until the sugar dissolves. Increase the heat and cook gently for 4–5 minutes until the mixture turns dark golden brown and is thick, but pourable. Pour evenly over the bottom of the cake pan.

3 Peel, core, and slice the apples. Toss them with the lemon zest and juice. Arrange in the cake pan (see box, right).

4 Preheat the oven to 400°F (200°C). Roll out the dough on a lightly floured surface into a round slightly larger than the pan. Lay the dough over the apples, tucking the excess down the side of the pan.

5 Bake for 25–30 minutes until the crust is crisp and golden. Invert a serving plate on top of the pan, turn the pan and plate over, and lift the pan to reveal the caramelized apples. Serve warm or cold with whipped cream.

Arranging the apples in the cake pan

Arrange a single layer of the best apple slices in a circular pattern on top of the caramel mixture. Cover evenly with the remaining apple slices.

French apple **tart**

 SERVES 10

Ingredients

DOUGH

2 cups all-purpose flour

9 tbsp chilled butter, cut into cubes

½ cup granulated sugar

4 large egg yolks

6 tbsp butter

PURÉE

3lb (1.5kg) tart apples, quartered, cored, and cut into chunks

3 tbsp water

6 tbsp apricot jam

½ cup granulated sugar

grated zest of 1 large lemon

APPLE TOPPING AND GLAZE

12oz (375g) sweet apples, quartered, cored, peeled, and sliced

juice of 1 lemon

1 tbsp granulated sugar

6 tbsp apricot jam

SPECIAL EQUIPMENT

11in (28cm) loose-bottomed fluted tart pan

baking beans

Method

1 Make the dough: put the flour into a bowl and rub in the butter until the mixture resembles fine bread crumbs. Stir in the sugar, then the egg yolks and a little cold water, if needed, to make a soft dough. Wrap and chill for 30 minutes.

2 Melt the butter in a large saucepan and add the tart apples and water. Cover and cook very gently for 20–25 minutes until the apples are soft.

3 Rub the apples through a nylon sieve into a clean pan. Add the jam, sugar, and lemon zest. Cook over high heat for 15–20 minutes, stirring constantly, until all the liquid has evaporated and the apple purée is thick. Let cool.

4 Preheat the oven to 375°F (190°C). Roll out the dough on a lightly floured surface and use to line the tart pan. Bake blind (page 13) for 10–15 minutes. Remove the beans and foil and bake for another 5 minutes. Cool.

5 Spoon the apple purée into the crust. Arrange the apple slices on top, brush with lemon juice, and sprinkle with granulated sugar. Return to the oven and bake for 30–35 minutes until the apples are tender and their edges lightly browned.

6 Heat the jam, work through a sieve, then brush over the apples. Serve the tart warm or cold.

Tarte au citron

 SERVES 10–12

Ingredients

DOUGH

2 cups all-purpose flour

9 tbsp chilled butter, cut into cubes

¼ cup granulated sugar

1 large egg

1–2 tbsp water

FILLING

9 large eggs

1¼ cups heavy cream

grated zest and juice of 5 large lemons

1½ cups granulated sugar

confectioners' sugar for dusting

lemon twists to decorate

SPECIAL EQUIPMENT

11in (28cm) loose-bottomed fluted tart pan

baking beans

Method

1 Make the dough: put the flour into a large bowl. Add the butter and rub in with your fingertips until the mixture resembles fine bread crumbs.

2 Stir in the granulated sugar, then bind together with the egg and water to make a soft, pliable dough. Wrap in plastic wrap and chill for 30 minutes.

3 Preheat the oven to 400°F (200°C). Roll out the dough on a lightly floured surface and use to line the tart pan. Bake blind (page 13) for 10 minutes.

4 Remove the baking beans and foil and bake the tart crust for 5 minutes or until the base has dried out. Remove from the oven and reduce the oven temperature to 350°F (180°C).

5 Beat the eggs in a bowl and add the cream, lemon zest and juice, and granulated sugar. Stir until smooth, and pour into the tart crust.

6 Bake for 35–40 minutes until the lemon filling has set. Cover the tart loosely with foil if the crust begins to brown too much.

7 Let the tart cool a little, then dust with confectioners' sugar. Decorate with lemon twists and serve warm or at room temperature.

So often the star of French pâtissèrie, this golden fruit tart is easy enough to make at home.

French apricot & almond pie

 SERVES 10

Ingredients

DOUGH

2 cups all-purpose flour

9 tbsp chilled butter, cut into cubes

¼ cup granulated sugar

1 large egg, beaten

1–2 tbsp water

TOPPING

2lb (1kg) fresh apricots, halved and pitted

juice of 1 lemon

½ cup water

¼ cup granulated sugar

crème pâtissière (see p15)

1 tsp arrowroot

1 tbsp brandy

¼ cup toasted sliced almonds

SPECIAL EQUIPMENT

11in (28cm) loose-bottomed fluted tart pan

baking beans

Method

1 Make the dough: sift the flour into a large bowl. Add the butter and rub in until the mixture resembles fine bread crumbs.

2 Stir in the sugar, then mix in the egg and water to make a soft, pliable dough. Wrap in plastic wrap and chill for 30 minutes.

3 Preheat the oven to 400°F (200°C). Roll out the dough on a lightly floured surface and use to line the tart pan. Bake blind (page 13) until the pie crust is beginning to brown at the edges. Remove the beans and foil and bake for another 5–10 minutes. Let cool.

4 Put the apricots, cut-side down, in a shallow pan with the lemon juice, measured water, and sugar. Cover tightly and bring to a boil. Lower the heat and simmer gently for 3 minutes or until just soft.

5 Remove the apricots with a slotted spoon, reserving the juices. Drain on paper towels and let cool.

6 Remove the pie crust from the tart pan and put on a serving plate. Spread the crème pâtissière over the pie crust and smooth the surface.

7 Arrange the apricots, cut-side down, on the crème pâtissière. Combine the arrowroot and brandy in a small bowl and stir in the reserved apricot juices.

8 Return the mixture to the pan and bring to a boil, stirring until thick. Add the toasted sliced almonds.

9 Spoon the glaze over the apricots, making sure they are evenly coated. (Add a little water to the glaze if it is too thick.) Let stand until the glaze has cooled and set. Serve the tart cold.

Apple **tarte** au citron

For image see p129

 SERVES 10

Ingredients

DOUGH

2 cups all-purpose flour

¼ cup confectioners' sugar

9 tbsp butter, cut into cubes

1 large egg, beaten

1–2 tbsp water

FILLING

4 large eggs

1 cup granulated sugar

finely grated zest and juice of 2 lemons

9 tbsp butter, melted

2 large tart apples, e.g. Macintosh, quartered, cored, and peeled—about 12oz (350g) prepared weight

2 red sweet apples, quartered, cored, and thinly sliced (leave the red skin on)

about 2 tbsp dark brown sugar

fresh whipping cream to serve

SPECIAL EQUIPMENT

deep 10in (25cm) loose-bottomed tart pan

Method

1 Make the dough: sift the flour and confectioners' sugar into a bowl and rub in the cubes of butter until the mixture resembles bread crumbs. Stir in the egg and water and bring together to form a dough. (If making the dough in a food processor, process the flour, butter, and confectioners' sugar until like bread crumbs, pour in the beaten egg, and pulse until the dough forms a ball.) Form the dough into a smooth ball, put into a plastic bag, and chill in the refrigerator for at least 30 minutes.

2 Roll out the chilled dough on a lightly floured surface and use to line the pan. Chill again for 30 minutes.

3 Place a baking sheet in the bottom third of the oven and preheat oven to 400°F (200°C). Prepare the filling: beat the eggs, granulated sugar, and lemon zest and juice in a bowl. Stir in the warm melted butter, then coarsely grate the tart apples directly into mixture and mix well.

4 Spread the runny lemon mixture in the chilled tart crust. Level the surface with the back of a spoon and arrange the red-skinned apples around the outside edge. Sprinkle with the dark brown sugar.

5 Bake on the hot baking sheet for about 40–50 minutes or until the center feels firm to the touch and the apples are tinged brown. Serve at once with fresh whipping cream.

Mississippi mud pie

 SERVES 12

Ingredients

DOUGH

2 cups all-purpose flour

9 tbsp chilled butter, cut into cubes

about 2–3 tbsp cold water

FILLING

7oz (200g) dark chocolate

9 tbsp butter

1 tbsp coffee extract

3 large eggs

⅔ cup half-and-half

1 cup dark brown sugar

⅔ cup whipping cream to decorate

SPECIAL EQUIPMENT

10in (25cm) loose-bottomed fluted tart pan

baking beans

Method

1 Make the dough: put the flour into a large bowl. Add the butter and rub in until the mixture resembles fine bread crumbs. Add enough cold water to make a soft, pliable dough.

2 Wrap the dough and chill for 30 minutes. Preheat the oven to 400°F (200°C).

3 Roll out the dough on a lightly floured surface and use to line the tart pan.

4 Bake the pie crust blind (page 13) for about 10 minutes until the edges begin to brown.

5 Remove the baking beans and foil and bake for another 5 minutes or until the base has dried out. Remove the pie crust from the oven and reduce the oven temperature to 375°F (190°C).

6 Break the chocolate into pieces and place in a heavy pan with the butter and coffee extract. Heat gently, stirring occasionally, until the chocolate and butter have melted. Remove from the heat. Let the mixture cool slightly.

7 Beat the eggs, then add to the saucepan with the half-and-half and sugar. Stir thoroughly to mix.

8 Pour the filling into the pie crust. Bake for 30–35 minutes until the filling has set. Let cool.

9 Carefully pipe whipped cream rosettes around the edge of the pie before serving.

Pecan pie

 SERVES 8

Ingredients

DOUGH

1⅓ cups all-purpose flour

6 tbsp chilled butter, cut into cubes

about 2 tbsp cold water

1 extra large egg white, lightly beaten

FILLING

1⅓ cups pecan halves

2 tbsp unsalted butter

⅓ cup light brown sugar

2 tbsp granulated sugar

½ cup corn syrup

3 tbsp brandy

1 tsp vanilla extract

2 tbsp half-and-half

¼ tsp ground cinnamon

pinch of grated nutmeg

1 large egg, lightly beaten

2 large egg yolks

SPECIAL EQUIPMENT

9in (23cm) loose-bottomed fluted tart pan

baking beans

Method

1 Make the dough: put the flour into a bowl, add the butter, and rub in with your fingertips until the mixture resembles fine bread crumbs. Add enough water to make a soft dough. Let chill for about 30 minutes.

2 Preheat the oven to 350°F (180°C). Roll out the dough on a lightly floured work surface and line the tart pan. Bake blind (page 13) for 10 minutes.

3 Remove the beans and foil, lightly brush the crust with egg white, and return to the oven for 1–2 minutes. Remove from the oven and set aside.

4 Spread the pecans out on a baking sheet and roast in the oven, turning occasionally, for 10–15 minutes. Reserve a few pecan halves and coarsely chop the remainder. Leave the oven on.

5 Put the butter in a heavy saucepan and cook over low heat until it turns golden brown. Add the sugars and corn syrup and heat gently until the sugars dissolve. Add the brandy, bring to a boil, and cook for 5 minutes.

6 Remove from the heat and stir in the vanilla extract, half-and-half, cinnamon, and nutmeg.

7 Whisk together the egg and egg yolks. Whisk a little hot brandy mixture into the eggs. Add half of the brandy mixture, little by little, then add the remainder. Let cool.

8 Arrange the chopped pecans and pecan halves in the pie base. Pour the egg mixture over them. Bake in the oven for about 40 minutes until golden brown and set. Let cool before serving.

Lemon meringue pie

 SERVES 8–10

Ingredients

DOUGH

2 cups all-purpose flour

¼ cup confectioners' sugar

9 tbsp chilled butter, cut into cubes

1 large egg yolk

2 tbsp cold water

FILLING

grated zest and juice of 4 large lemons

¾ cup cornstarch

2½ cups water

4 large egg yolks

⅔ cup granulated sugar

MERINGUE

5 large egg whites

1 cup granulated sugar

SPECIAL EQUIPMENT

10in (25cm) loose-bottomed fluted tart pan

baking beans

Method

1 Make the dough: sift the flour and confectioners' sugar into a large bowl. Add the butter and rub in with your fingertips until the mixture resembles fine bread crumbs.

2 Mix in the egg yolk and enough cold water to make a soft, pliable dough. Wrap the dough in plastic wrap and chill in the refrigerator for about 30 minutes.

3 Preheat the oven to 400°F (200°C). Roll out the dough on a lightly floured surface and use to line the tart pan. Bake blind (page 13) for 10 minutes.

4 Remove the baking beans and foil and bake the pie crust for 5 minutes or until the base has dried out. Remove from the oven and reduce the temperature to 300°F (150°C).

5 Mix the lemon zest and juice with the cornstarch. Bring the water to a boil, then stir into the lemon mixture. Beat the egg yolks with the granulated sugar.

6 Let cool slightly, then stir in the egg yolk mixture and whisk until smooth. Pour into the pie crust.

7 Beat the egg whites with a hand-held electric mixer on maximum speed until stiff but not dry. Beat in the sugar 1 tsp at a time. Pile on top of the filling and spread over evenly. Bake for 45 minutes or until crisp and brown. Serve the pie warm or cold.

Key lime pie

 SERVES 8

Ingredients

DOUGH

1⅓ cups all-purpose flour

6 tbsp chilled butter, cut into cubes

about 2 tbsp cold water

FILLING

1¼ cups heavy cream

1 x 14oz (400g) can full-fat sweetened condensed milk

grated zest and juice of 1 lime

lime slices to decorate

SPECIAL EQUIPMENT

9in (23cm) loose-bottomed fluted tart pan

baking beans

Method

1 Make the dough: put the flour into a large bowl, add the butter, and rub in until the mixture resembles fine bread crumbs. Add enough cold water to make a soft, pliable dough.

2 Wrap the dough in plastic wrap or foil and chill in the refrigerator for 30 minutes. Preheat the oven to 400°F (200°C).

3 Roll out the dough on a lightly floured surface and use to line the tart pan.

4 Bake the pie crust blind (page 13) for about 10 minutes. Remove the baking beans and foil and return the crust to the oven for 5 minutes. Cool slightly.

5 Whip the cream to soft peaks in a large bowl and mix together with the condensed milk. Slowly stir in the lime zest and juice until the mixture thickens.

6 Pour the mixture into the pie crust and smooth the top, or create a pattern with a palette knife. Chill in the refrigerator for at least 2 hours or until the filling is set firm.

7 Serve the pie chilled, decorated with lime slices.

Plum & almond **tart**

 SERVES 6

Ingredients

DOUGH

2 cups all-purpose flour

1 cup confectioners' sugar, sifted

9 tbsp butter, cut into cubes

1 small egg, beaten

1–2 tbsp water

a little milk for glazing

FILLING

6oz (175g) golden marzipan, grated

1lb (500g) ripe plums, halved and pitted

confectioners' sugar for sifting

SPECIAL EQUIPMENT

9in (23cm) fluted tart pan

Method

1 Put a baking sheet in the oven and preheat the oven to 400°F (200°C).

2 Make the dough: put the flour, sugar, and butter into a food processor and pulse until the mixture resembles fine bread crumbs. Add the egg and pulse again until the dough holds together in a ball. (To make by hand, put the flour into a bowl and rub in the butter with your fingertips, then stir in the sugar, egg, and water.) Knead the dough on a lightly floured surface until smooth, then wrap in plastic wrap and chill for 10 minutes.

3 Remove a little less than half of the dough for the top of the tart and return it to the refrigerator. Roll out the remaining dough on a lightly floured surface and use to line the bottom and sides of the tart pan, making a rim around the top edge. If the dough cracks, press it together again, and patch it with rolled-out dough trimmings if necessary.

4 Prick all over the bottom of the dough with a fork and scatter with the grated marzipan. Arrange the plums cut-side down on top. Brush the rim with water. Roll out the reserved dough to a round that is slightly larger than the diameter of the pan and place over the plums. Press the dough edges together to seal, and trim off any excess. Brush with a little milk to glaze.

5 Place the pan on the hot baking sheet and bake for 30–35 minutes until pale golden. Sift confectioners' sugar over the tart and serve warm.

Raspberry tartlets

For image see p121

 MAKES 16

Ingredients

DOUGH

2 cups all-purpose flour

9 tbsp chilled butter, cut into cubes

2 tbsp granulated sugar

3–4 tbsp cold water

FILLING

8oz (250g) full-fat mascarpone

2 tbsp granulated sugar

12oz (350g) raspberries

3 tbsp red currant jelly

1–2 tsp lemon juice to taste

SPECIAL EQUIPMENT

3in (7cm) pastry cutter

16 x 2½in (6cm) round tartlet pans

Method

1 Make the dough: put the flour into a bowl, add the butter, and rub in with your fingertips until the mixture resembles fine bread crumbs. Stir in the sugar, then add enough cold water to bind to a soft pliable dough. Wrap and chill for at least 30 minutes.

2 On a lightly floured surface, roll out the dough thinly. Using the pastry cutter, cut out 16 rounds. Preheat the oven to 375°F (190°C).

3 Gently press the rounds into the tartlet pans. Prick all over with a fork and bake for 12–15 minutes until golden. Leave in the pans for 10 minutes, then remove and transfer to a wire rack. Let cool completely.

4 Beat together the mascarpone and sugar and spoon into the tartlet crusts. Top with the raspberries, pressing them gently into the filling.

5 Melt the jelly with lemon juice to taste in a small pan, then spoon over the fruits. Let set before serving.

Tropical tartlets

For image see p121

 MAKES 10

Ingredients

ALMOND DOUGH

½ cup ground almonds

1 cup all-purpose flour

2 tbsp granulated sugar

6 tbsp chilled butter, cut into cubes

about 3 tbsp cold water

1¼ cups store-bought vanilla pudding

1 x 7oz (200g) can mandarin oranges in natural juice, well-drained

1 x 7oz (200g) can apricot halves in natural juice, well-drained and cut into pieces

about 3 tbsp apricot jam

about ⅓ cup toasted sliced almonds

SPECIAL EQUIPMENT

10 x 3in (7cm) round tartlet pans or boat-shaped pans (barquette molds)

Method

1 Make the dough: combine the almonds, flour, and sugar in a bowl. Add the butter and rub in with your fingertips until the mixture resembles fine bread crumbs. Add enough cold water to make a soft, pliable dough. Wrap and chill for 1 hour.

2 Put the dough on a floured surface and flatten slightly. Place a large sheet of parchment paper on top and roll out the dough, beneath the parchment, until about ⅛in (3mm) thick. Line the tartlet pans with dough and chill for 2 hours. Preheat the oven to 375°F (190°C).

3 Prick the dough all over and bake for 10 minutes. Let the shells cool in the pans for 10 minutes. Remove and transfer to a wire rack to cool.

4 Spoon the vanilla pudding into each shell, then top with the mandarin oranges and apricots. Melt the jam in a small pan, sieve, then spoon over the fruit. Sprinkle with the almonds and let set before serving.

Blueberry **puffs**

 MAKES 8

Ingredients

1lb (500g) store-bought puff pastry

1 large egg, beaten

4oz (100g) blueberries

⅔ cup heavy or whipping cream

1 tbsp granulated sugar

1 ripe nectarine or peach, pitted and sliced

confectioners' sugar for dusting

Method

1 Preheat the oven to 450°F (230°C). Roll out the pastry until ¼in (5mm) thick on a lightly floured surface. Cut into strips 3in (7cm) wide, then cut the strips diagonally into 8 diamond shapes.

2 With a sharp knife, score each pastry diamond ½in (1cm) from the edge, being careful not to cut all the way through. Place on a dampened baking sheet and glaze with beaten egg.

3 Bake for 10–15 minutes until golden. Transfer to a wire rack. Remove the pastry centers, reserving them for lids if desired. Let cool.

4 Divide half of the blueberries among the pastry shells. Whip the cream and sugar and divide among the shells. Top with nectarine or peach slices, and the remaining blueberries. Dust the pastry lids with confectioners' sugar, replace, and serve.

Opposite, clockwise from top: Raspberry tartlets (p118), Blueberry puffs, Tropical tartlets (p119).

This is also very good made with thinly sliced unpeeled sweet apples instead of apricots. Use about three per galette. Serve warm with cream.

Apricot & almond galette

MAKES 2 (SERVES 12)

Ingredients

a little all-purpose flour, for dusting

1 x 13oz (375g) package all-butter puff pastry

a little milk

2 x 14oz (400g) cans apricots in natural juices, drained

9oz (250g) golden marzipan, coarsely grated

2 tbsp apricot jam

2 tsp water

Method

1 Preheat the oven to 425°F (220°C). Pop a baking sheet in to get hot. Lightly flour a piece of parchment paper and roll the pastry out into a 10 x 12in (25 x 30cm) rectangle, cut it in half lengthwise to make two strips, then arrange them neatly side by side.

2 With a knife, score a ½in (1cm) border around the rectangles, being careful not to cut all the way through—this allows the strip to rise up around the apricots and keeps any liquid or fruit from leaking out. Brush the borders with a little milk.

3 Slice each apricot into four slices and arrange them in rows inside the borders. Sprinkle with the marzipan.

4 Slide the paper onto the hot baking sheet and bake for 20–25 minutes or until golden brown. Check halfway through cooking and, if they are getting too brown, cover loosely with foil.

5 Heat the apricot jam in a pan with the water, whisking until smooth. Brush the apricots with a thin layer to glaze them. Serve warm.

These individual crumbles are scrumptious and so easy to make.
Serve with cream, crème fraîche, or warm pouring custard.

Mini apple, apricot, & hazelnut **crumbles**

 SERVES 6

Ingredients

2lb (900g) Macintosh apples, peeled and cut into ½in (1cm) cubes

6oz (175g) ready-to-eat dried apricots, cut into small pieces

½ cup apple juice

1 heaping tbsp dark brown sugar

TOPPING

¾ cup all-purpose flour

3 tbsp cold butter, cut into cubes

½ cup dark brown sugar

¼ cup hazelnuts, chopped

SPECIAL EQUIPMENT

6 x size 1 (5fl oz/150ml) ramekins

Method

1 Preheat the oven to 400°F (200°C). Put the apples, apricots, apple juice, and the dark brown sugar into a saucepan. Bring to a boil, cover with a lid, and simmer for 5–7 minutes or until the apples are just soft. Remove from the heat and divide among the ramekins.

2 Make the topping: put the flour and butter into a mixing bowl and rub together. Add the sugar and the hazelnuts and mix together.

3 Sprinkle the crumble topping over the apples in the ramekins, then place on a baking sheet and bake for 15 minutes or until the crumble is light golden brown and the fruit is bubbling around the edges.

Classic apple crumble

For image see p129

 SERVES 6

Ingredients

2lb (900g) tart apples, e.g. Macintosh

⅔ cup granulated sugar

finely grated zest of 1 lemon

6 tbsp water

TOPPING

1½ cups all-purpose flour

6 tbsp butter

⅓ cup dark brown sugar

SPECIAL EQUIPMENT

shallow 8in (20cm) ovenproof dish

🥄 Cook's know-how

For a crunchier topping on the classic apple crumble, use 1 cup whole wheat flour and ½ cup rolled oats instead of the all-purpose flour. To sweeten tart apples, especially windfall apples that are not at their best, use apricot jam instead of some— or all—of the sugar. Apricot jam gives a gentle sweetness, and it improves the texture of the apples, especially if you are using them for a purée or a pie.

Method

1 Preheat the oven to 350°F (180°C). Quarter, peel, and core the apples, then slice them fairly thinly. Toss the slices in the sugar, lemon zest, and water. Put in the dish.

2 Make the topping: put the flour in a bowl and rub in the butter until the mixture resembles fine bread crumbs, then stir in the sugar.

3 Sprinkle the topping evenly over the apple mixture in the dish and bake for 40–45 minutes until golden brown and bubbling. Serve at once.

Plum **crumble**

 SERVES 6

Ingredients

2lb (1kg) plums, halved and pitted

⅓ cup light brown sugar

1 tsp ground cinnamon

TOPPING

1¾ cups whole wheat flour

9 tbsp butter

½ cup light brown sugar

Method

1 Preheat the oven to 350°F (180°C). Put the plums into a shallow, ovenproof dish and sprinkle with the sugar and cinnamon.

2 Make the topping: put the flour into a bowl and rub in the butter with your fingertips until the mixture resembles fine bread crumbs. Stir in the sugar.

3 Sprinkle the topping evenly over the plums, without pressing it down, and bake for 30–40 minutes until golden. Serve the crumble hot.

Crunchy apricot crumble

Substitute fresh apricots for the plums, and omit the cinnamon. Substitute rolled oats for half of the flour in the crumble topping, or use up to 1¼ cups chopped toasted hazelnuts. You can also use half white and half whole wheat flour.

Rhubarb and ginger crumble

Substitute 2lb (1kg) rhubarb, cut into 1in (2.5cm) pieces, for the plums. Put into a saucepan with the sugar, 2 tbsp water, and 1 tsp ground ginger instead of the cinnamon, and cook gently until the rhubarb is soft.

Blackberry & apple **cobbler**

 SERVES 4

Ingredients

2 tart apples, e.g. Macintosh

1lb (500g) blackberries

¼ cup granulated sugar

finely grated zest and juice of 1 lemon

TOPPING

2 cups self-rising flour

4 tbsp butter, cubed

⅓ cup granulated sugar

⅓ cup milk, plus extra for glazing

SPECIAL EQUIPMENT

2in (5cm) round fluted cookie cutter

Method

1 Preheat oven to 425°F (225°C). Quarter, peel, and core the apples, then cut the apples into large slices, about ½in (1cm) thick.

2 Put the apples into a saucepan with the blackberries, sugar, and lemon zest and juice. Cover and simmer gently for 10–15 minutes until the apple pieces are tender but not broken up.

3 Meanwhile, make the cobbler topping: put the flour into a bowl, add the cubes of butter, and rub in with your fingertips until the mixture resembles fine bread crumbs. Stir in the sugar, add the milk, and mix to form a soft dough.

4 Roll out the dough on a lightly floured surface until ½in (1cm) thick. Cut out as many shapes as you can with the cookie cutter, then re-roll the trimmings and cut out more. If you do not have a cookie cutter, stamp out rounds with the rim of a glass or coffee mug.

5 Transfer the fruit to an ovenproof dish, arrange the dough shapes on top, and brush with milk to glaze.

6 Bake for 15–20 minutes until the cobbler topping is golden. Serve at once.

Opposite, clockwise from top right:
Classic apple crumble (p125), Apple tarte au citron (p108), Blackberry and apple cobbler

Apple **strudel**

 SERVES 8

Ingredients

four 10 x 18in (25 x 45cm) sheets
of filo dough

4 tbsp butter, melted

½ cup fresh white bread crumbs

3 tbsp sliced almonds

confectioners' sugar for dusting

FILLING

1½lb (750g) tart apples, quartered,
cored, peeled, and sliced

grated zest and juice of 1 lemon

3 tbsp light brown sugar

½ tsp ground pumpkin pie spice

½ tsp ground cinnamon

¾ cup golden raisins

⅓ cup blanched almonds,
roughly chopped

Method

1 Preheat the oven to 375°F (190°C). Make the filling: mix together the apples, lemon zest and juice, sugar, pumpkin pie spice, cinnamon, golden raisins, and almonds.

2 Lightly brush 1 sheet of filo dough with melted butter. Cover with the remaining sheets, brushing each with butter. Add the filling and finish the strudel (see box, below).

3 Brush the strudel with the remaining melted butter and sprinkle with the almonds. Bake for 40–45 minutes until the dough is crisp and golden. Dust with confectioners' sugar. Serve warm or cold.

Finishing the strudel

Sprinkle the bread crumbs over the dough. Spoon the apple mixture along the middle of the dough.

Fold the dough to enclose the filling, turn over onto a baking sheet, and bend into a horseshoe shape.

British favorites

Devon **scones**

 MAKES 12

Ingredients

4 tbsp chilled butter, cubed, plus extra for greasing

1¾ cups self-rising flour

2½ tbsp granulated sugar

1 large egg

about ⅔ cup milk, plus extra for glazing

butter and jam to serve

SPECIAL EQUIPMENT

2in (5cm) pastry cutter

Method

1 Preheat the oven to 425°F (220°C). Lightly butter a large baking sheet.

2 Sift the flour into a bowl. Rub in the butter with your fingertips until the mixture resembles fine bread crumbs. Stir in the sugar.

3 Break the egg into a liquid measuring cup and make up to ⅔ cup with milk. Beat lightly to mix. Add to the bowl and mix to a soft dough.

4 Lightly knead the dough on a floured work surface until smooth. Roll out until ½in (1cm) thick, cut into rounds with the pastry cutter, and put on the baking sheet. Reroll the scraps and continue cutting until all the dough is used. Brush with milk.

5 Bake for about 10 minutes until risen and golden. Cool on a wire rack. Serve on the day of making, if possible, with butter and jam.

Cheese scones

Omit the sugar, and add 4oz (125g) grated aged cheddar cheese and ½ tsp mustard powder to the dry ingredients before mixing in the egg and milk. Roll out the dough into a 6in (15cm) round and cut it into wedges. Brush with milk and sprinkle with finely grated cheese. Bake as directed.

Welsh cakes

 MAKES 12

Ingredients

1¾ cups self-rising flour

9 tbsp butter

½ cup granulated sugar

½ cup currants

½ tsp ground pumpkin pie spice

1 large egg, beaten

about 2 tbsp milk

sunflower oil for greasing

SPECIAL EQUIPMENT

3in (7cm) pastry cutter

Method

1 Sift the flour into a large bowl. Add the butter and rub in with your fingertips until the mixture resembles fine bread crumbs.

2 Add the sugar, currants, and pumpkin pie spice and stir to mix. Add the egg and enough milk to form a soft, but not sticky, dough.

3 On a lightly floured work surface, roll out the dough to a thickness of ¼in (5mm). Cut into rounds with a pastry cutter.

4 Heat a flat griddle pan or a heavy frying pan and grease with a little oil. Cook the Welsh cakes on the hot pan over low heat for about 3 minutes on each side until cooked through and golden brown.

5 Let cool on a wire rack. Serve on the day of making, if possible.

Seeded bars are extremely popular in many coffee shops. They are also healthier than a slice of cake, so why not make your own? When I was testing these, the whole lot went in one go!

Figgy seeded bites

 MAKES 12 BARS OR 24 BITES

Ingredients

5 tbsp butter

2 tbsp golden syrup or 1 tbsp corn syrup and 1 tbsp honey

½ cup granulated sugar

2 cups rolled oats

¼ cup sunflower seeds

¼ cup pumpkin seeds

½ cup shredded coconut

¾ cup dried figs, sliced into tiny pieces

¼ cup dried apricots, sliced into tiny pieces

SPECIAL EQUIPMENT

7in (8cm) square shallow pan, lined with parchment paper and greased

Method

1 Preheat the oven to 350°F (180°C). Heat the butter, syrup, and sugar in a pan over gentle heat, stirring until melted and dissolved.

2 Put the remaining ingredients into a large mixing bowl, add the melted butter mixture, and stir well. Pour into the pan and level the top.

3 Bake for 30–35 minutes or until lightly golden and firm in the middle. Let cool slightly, then cut into 12 rectangles or 24 squares. Leave in the pan to harden, then transfer to a wire rack to cool completely.

Wimbledon cake

 CUTS INTO 8 SLICES

Ingredients

butter for greasing

3 large eggs

½ cup granulated sugar

½ cup self-rising flour

FILLING AND TOPPING

1¼ cups whipping cream, whipped until thick

4oz (125g) strawberries, sliced

1 passion fruit, halved

strawberries, halved, to decorate

SPECIAL EQUIPMENT

2 x 7in (18cm) round cake pans

Method

1 Preheat the oven to 375°F (190°C). Lightly butter the cake pans, line the bottoms with parchment paper, then butter the parchment.

2 Put the eggs and sugar into a large bowl. Beat with an electric mixer at high speed until the mixture is pale and thick enough to leave a trail when the beaters are lifted out.

3 Sift in half of the flour and fold in gently. Repeat with the remaining flour.

4 Divide the mixture between the pans. Tilt to spread the mixture evenly.

5 Bake for 20–25 minutes until well-risen, golden, and beginning to shrink away from the sides of the pans. Turn onto a wire rack, peel off the lining paper, and let cool.

6 Spread half of the whipped cream over 1 of the cakes. Top with the sliced strawberries and passion fruit pulp. Put the other cake on top and press down gently.

7 Spread the remaining cream on top of the cake, smoothing it neatly with a palette knife. Decorate with strawberry halves.

Victoria layer cake

 CUTS INTO 8 SLICES

Ingredients

12 tbsp soft butter or margarine, plus extra for greasing

⅔ cup granulated sugar

3 large eggs

1½ cups self-rising flour

1½ tsp baking powder

FILLING

¼ cup raspberry or strawberry jam

granulated sugar for sprinkling

SPECIAL EQUIPMENT

2 x 7in (18cm) round cake pans

Method

1 Preheat the oven to 350°F (180°C). Lightly grease the pans and line the bottoms with parchment paper.

2 Combine all the cake ingredients in a large bowl. Beat well for about 2 minutes until smooth.

3 Divide the mixture between the prepared pans and level the surfaces. Bake for about 25 minutes or until the cakes are well-risen, golden, and springy to the touch.

4 Turn onto a wire rack, peel off the lining paper, and let cool.

5 Sandwich the 2 cakes together with jam and sprinkle the top of the cake with granulated sugar.

Lemon layer cake

Add the finely grated zest of 1 lemon to the cake ingredients before beating. Sandwich the cakes together with ¼ cup lemon curd and ½ cup whipping cream, whipped until thick. Dust with sifted confectioners' sugar.

Dundee cake

 CUTS INTO 12 SLICES

Ingredients

10 tbsp butter, at room temperature, plus extra for greasing

1 cup light brown sugar

3 large eggs

1¾ cups all-purpose flour

1 tsp baking powder

1 cup golden raisins

½ cup currants

½ cup raisins

⅓ cup glacé cherries, quartered, rinsed, and dried

½ cup chopped mixed candied peel

2 tbsp ground almonds

grated zest of 1 large lemon

½ cup whole almonds, blanched and halved, to decorate

SPECIAL EQUIPMENT

deep 8in (20cm) round loose-bottomed cake pan

Method

1 Preheat the oven to 325°F (160°C). Lightly butter the cake pan and line the bottom with parchment paper.

2 Combine the butter, sugar, eggs, flour, and baking powder in a bowl and beat for 2 minutes or until well-blended. Stir in the fruit, mixed peel, ground almonds, and lemon zest.

3 Spoon the mixture into the prepared pan. Level the surface and arrange the halved almonds neatly in concentric circles on top.

4 Bake for 1½ hours or until well-risen, golden, and firm to the touch. A fine skewer inserted into the middle of the cake should come out clean. Cover the cake with foil halfway through baking if it is browning too quickly.

5 Let the cake cool in the pan for a few minutes, then turn onto a wire rack and let cool completely. Store in an airtight container for about 1 week before eating.

Treacle **tart**

 SERVES 8

Ingredients

DOUGH

1½ cups all-purpose flour

6 tbsp chilled butter, cut into cubes

about 2 tbsp cold water

1 cup golden syrup or ½ cup corn syrup plus ½ cup honey

about 2 cups fresh white or brown bread crumbs

grated zest and juice of 1 large lemon

SPECIAL EQUIPMENT

10in (25cm) loose-bottomed fluted tart pan

Method

1 Make the dough: put the flour into a large bowl, add the butter, and rub in with your fingertips until the mixture resembles fine bread crumbs. Mix in enough water to make a soft, pliable dough.

2 Wrap the dough in plastic wrap and chill in the refrigerator for about 30 minutes.

3 Preheat the oven to 400°F (200°C). Roll out the dough on a lightly floured surface and use to line the tart pan.

4 Gently heat the syrup in a saucepan until melted, and stir in the bread crumbs and lemon zest and juice. Pour into the tart crust.

5 Bake for 10 minutes; reduce the oven temperature to 350°F (180°C), and bake for another 30 minutes or until the tart is golden and the filling firm.

6 Let cool in the pan for a few minutes. Serve warm, cut into slices with a spoonful of cream and a little grated lemon zest.

Bakewell tart

 SERVES 6

Ingredients

DOUGH

1½ cups all-purpose flour

6 tbsp chilled butter, cut into cubes

about 2 tbsp cold water

milk for glazing

9 tbsp butter

½ cup granulated sugar

1 large egg, lightly beaten

¾ cup rice flour or semolina

½ tsp almond extract

2 tbsp raspberry jam

confectioners' sugar for dusting

SPECIAL EQUIPMENT

7½in (19cm) loose-bottomed fluted tart pan

Method

1 Make the dough: put the flour into a large bowl. Rub in the butter until the mixture resembles fine bread crumbs. Mix in enough water to make a soft, pliable dough. Wrap in plastic wrap and chill for 30 minutes.

2 Preheat the oven to 400°F (200°C). Roll out the dough on a lightly floured work surface and use to line the tart pan. Reserve the trimmings.

3 Melt the butter in a saucepan, stir in the granulated sugar, and cook for about 1 minute. Remove from the heat, let cool a little, then gradually stir in the egg, rice flour or semolina, and almond extract.

4 Spread the jam evenly over the bottom of the tart crust, and pour the almond mixture on top.

5 Roll out the reserved trimmings and cut into thin strips, long enough to fit across the tart. Arrange the strips on top of the almond filling to form a lattice, attaching them to the edge of the tart crust with a little milk.

6 Bake for 45–50 minutes until the filling is well-risen and golden and springs back when lightly pressed with a finger. If the crust is browning too much, cover the tart loosely with foil.

7 Remove the tart from the oven. Sprinkle with confectioners' sugar and serve the tart warm or cold.

Banoffi **pie**

 SERVES 8

Ingredients

6 tbsp butter, plus extra for greasing

½ cup light brown sugar

1 x 14oz (400g) can dulce de leche

GRAHAM CRACKER CRUST

6 tbsp butter

1¾ cups graham crackers, crushed

TOPPING

2 bananas

⅔ cup heavy or whipping cream, lightly whipped

cocoa powder or chocolate curls to decorate

SPECIAL EQUIPMENT

8in (20cm) springform or loose-bottomed cake pan

Method

1 Lightly grease the cake pan and line with parchment paper.

2 Make the graham cracker crust: melt the butter in a saucepan, add the crushed graham crackers, and stir well to combine. Press onto the bottom and sides of the tart pan. Place in the refrigerator to set.

3 Meanwhile, make the filling: put the butter and sugar into a saucepan and stir over low heat until melted and combined. Add the dulce de leche and stir until smooth. Bring to a boil over high heat, stirring. Boil for 1 minute only, then pour immediately over the crust in the pan. Chill for at least 30 minutes, until set. (The pie can be made up to this stage the day before serving.)

4 Make the topping: peel the bananas, cut into chunky slices, and arrange over the set toffee base. Spread the whipped cream over the bananas to cover them completely so they do not discolor. Chill the pie for at least 2 hours until firm enough to cut (it will keep in the refrigerator for up to 6 hours). Before serving, sift cocoa powder over the cream or decorate with chocolate curls.

Eve's pudding

 SERVES 4

Ingredients

butter for greasing

1lb (500g) tart apples, quartered, cored, peeled, and sliced

½ cup dark brown sugar

grated zest and juice of 1 lemon

TOPPING

9 tbsp margarine, straight from the refrigerator

½ cup granulated sugar

2 large eggs, beaten

1 cup self-rising flour

SPECIAL EQUIPMENT

1-quart baking dish

Method

1 Preheat the oven to 350°F (180°C). Lightly butter the ovenproof dish and arrange the apples in the bottom. Sprinkle with the dark brown sugar and the lemon zest and juice.

2 Make the cake topping: put the margarine, sugar, eggs, and flour in a large bowl and beat until smooth and well-blended. Spoon on top of the apple slices and level the surface.

3 Bake for about 45 minutes until the cake topping is well-risen, golden, and springy to the touch. Serve hot.

Spiced Eve's pudding

Add 1 tsp ground cinnamon to the cake topping, and ⅓ cup raisins, 1 tsp ground cinnamon, and 1 tsp ground pumpkin pie spice to the apple mixture.

Queen of puddings

 SERVES 4

Ingredients

4 large egg yolks

2½ cups milk

2 tbsp butter, plus extra for greasing

⅓ cup granulated sugar

grated zest of 1 orange

1 cup fresh white bread crumbs

3 tbsp strawberry or raspberry jam

MERINGUE

4 large egg whites

⅔ cup granulated sugar

SPECIAL EQUIPMENT

shallow 1-quart baking dish

Method

1 In a large bowl, lightly beat the egg yolks. Set aside. Heat the milk in a small saucepan until bubbles appear around the edges. Add the butter, sugar, and orange zest, and heat gently until the butter has melted and the sugar dissolved.

2 Preheat the oven to 350°F (180°C). Lightly butter the baking dish and set aside. Gradually add the hot milk mixture to the egg yolks, whisking all the time.

3 Stir in the bread crumbs, then pour into the baking dish. Let stand for 15 minutes.

4 Bake the pudding for about 30 minutes until just set. Remove from the oven and set aside.

5 Warm the jam in a small saucepan until melted. Spread the warmed jam evenly over the surface of the pudding.

6 Make the meringue topping: whisk the egg whites until stiff but not dry. With an electric mixer, beat in the granulated sugar, 1 tsp at a time, keeping the mixer at full speed.

7 Spoon the meringue on top of the pudding, spreading it to the edges and pulling it up to form peaks.

8 Return the pudding to the oven and bake for another 10–15 minutes until the top of the meringue is crisp and golden brown. Serve at once.

Treacle pudding

 SERVES 4–6

Ingredients

8 tbsp grated chilled butter, plus extra for greasing

⅓ cup golden syrup or 2½ tbsp corn syrup plus 2½ tbsp honey

1 cup self-rising flour

1½ cups fresh white bread crumbs

⅓ cup granulated sugar

about ½ cup milk

SPECIAL EQUIPMENT

3-cup pudding bowl

Pouring custard

Heat 1¼ cups of milk in a pan until hot. Turn off the heat and add 1 vanilla bean, split open. Cover and infuse for 20 minutes. In a bowl, whisk 3 extra large egg yolks, 2 tbsp granulated sugar, and 1 tsp cornstarch until combined. Remove the vanilla bean. Whisk the milk into the egg yolk mixture. Return to the pan and stir over low heat with a wooden spoon. Cook for about 5 minutes, stirring constantly, until the custard is smooth and coats the back of the spoon.

Method

1 Lightly butter the bowl and spoon the syrup and honey into the bottom.

2 Put the butter, flour, bread crumbs, and sugar into a bowl and stir to combine. Stir in enough milk to give a dropping consistency. Spoon into the bowl on top of the syrup.

3 Cover the bowl with buttered parchment paper and foil, both pleated in the middle. Secure by tying string under the rim of the bowl (page 14).

4 Put the bowl into a steamer or saucepan of simmering water, making sure the water comes halfway up the sides of the bowl if using a saucepan. Cover and steam, adding more boiling water as needed, for about 3 hours. Turn out the pudding and serve with vanilla ice cream or the traditional British way—with pouring custard (see left).

Sticky toffee pudding

 SERVES 8

Ingredients

6 tbsp butter, softened, plus extra for greasing

1 cup light brown sugar

2 large eggs, beaten

1 tbsp coffee extract

1½ cups self-rising flour

1 cup pitted dates, coarsely chopped

1 cup walnuts, coarsely chopped

¾ cup hot water

TOFFEE SAUCE

9 tbsp butter

1¼ cups light brown sugar

6 tbsp heavy cream

¾ cup walnuts, coarsely chopped

SPECIAL EQUIPMENT

deep 8in (20cm) square cake pan

Method

1 Preheat the oven to 350°F (180°C). Butter the cake pan and line the bottom with parchment paper.

2 Put the butter, sugar, eggs, coffee extract, and flour into a large bowl. Beat well until smooth and thoroughly blended.

3 Stir in the dates and walnuts, and then the measured hot water. Pour the mixture into the pan.

4 Bake for 45–50 minutes until the pudding is well-risen, browned on top, and springy to the touch.

5 About 10 minutes before the pudding is ready, make the toffee sauce: put the butter and sugar into a small saucepan and heat gently, stirring, until the butter has melted and the sugar dissolved. Stir in the cream and walnuts and heat gently to warm through.

6 Cut the pudding into 8 even-sized squares and transfer to serving plates. Spoon over the toffee sauce and serve at once.

This is a rich, dark pudding, laden with dried fruit, spices, and alcohol—the traditional British way to finish the festive meal.

Christmas pudding

 SERVES 8–10

Ingredients

½ cup self-rising flour

8 tbsp grated chilled butter, plus extra for greasing

¼ cup blanched almonds, shredded

2 medium carrots, grated

1¼ cups raisins

1 cup currants

¾ cup golden raisins

1¼ cups fresh bread crumbs

¼ tsp grated nutmeg

½ cup mixed candied peel, chopped

½ cup light brown sugar

grated zest and juice of 1 lemon

2 large eggs, beaten

⅓ cup dark rum or brandy

brandy butter (see box, below) to serve

SPECIAL EQUIPMENT

1-quart pudding bowl

Method

1 In a large bowl, combine the flour, butter, almonds, carrots, raisins, currants, golden raisins, bread crumbs, nutmeg, candied peel, sugar, and lemon zest. Add the lemon juice and eggs, and stir until well-combined.

2 Lightly butter the pudding bowl. Spoon in the pudding mixture and level the surface.

3 Cover with buttered parchment paper, then foil, both pleated in the middle. Secure the paper and foil in place by tying string under the rim of the bowl (page 14).

4 Put the bowl into a steamer or saucepan of simmering water, making sure the water comes halfway up the sides of the bowl. Cover and steam, adding more boiling water as needed, for about 6 hours.

5 Remove the bowl from the steamer or pan and let cool. Remove the paper and foil covering. Make a few holes in the pudding with a fine skewer and pour in the rum or brandy.

6 Cover the pudding with fresh parchment paper and foil. Store in a cool place for up to 3 months. To reheat for serving, steam the pudding for 2–3 hours. Serve at once with brandy butter.

🔎 Brandy butter

Make your own brandy butter by creaming together 16 tbsp unsalted butter, 1 cup granulated sugar or confectioners' sugar, and ⅓ cup brandy. The brandy butter can be frozen for up to 3 months.

Steamed jam **pudding**

 SERVES 4–6

Ingredients

9 tbsp soft butter or margarine, plus extra for greasing

3 tbsp jam

½ cup granulated sugar

2 large eggs, beaten

1¼ cups self-rising flour

1 tsp baking powder

about 3 tbsp milk

SPECIAL EQUIPMENT

1-quart pudding bowl

Method

1 Lightly grease the pudding bowl and spoon the jam into the bottom.

2 Put the butter or margarine, sugar, eggs, flour, and baking powder into a large bowl, and beat until smooth and thoroughly blended. Add enough milk to give a dropping consistency.

3 Spoon the mixture into the pudding bowl and smooth the surface. Cover with greased parchment paper and foil, both pleated in the middle. Secure with string (page 14).

4 Put the bowl into a steamer or saucepan of simmering water, making sure the water comes halfway up the sides of the bowl. Cover and steam, adding more boiling water as needed, for about 2 hours or until it is a light, fluffy sponge all the way through. Turn the pudding onto a warmed plate and serve hot with pouring custard (see p150).

Magic chocolate pudding

 SERVES 4

Ingredients

⅓ **cup granulated sugar**

⅓ **cup fine semolina**

⅓ **cup cocoa powder**

1 **tsp baking powder**

2 **tbsp butter, melted, plus extra for greasing**

2 **large eggs, beaten**

2–3 **drops of vanilla extract**

confectioners' sugar for dusting

SAUCE

½ **cup light brown sugar**

2 **tbsp cocoa powder**

1¼ **cups hot water**

SPECIAL EQUIPMENT

1-**quart baking dish**

Method

1 Mix together the sugar and semolina in a large bowl. Sift the cocoa powder and baking powder into the bowl and mix thoroughly.

2 In a separate bowl, beat together the melted butter, eggs, and vanilla extract with a hand-held mixer. Add this mixture to the dry ingredients and stir with a wooden spoon until well-blended.

3 Preheat the oven to 350°F (180°C). Lightly butter the baking dish. Pour the mixture into the dish.

4 Make the sauce: mix together the brown sugar and cocoa powder, and gradually stir in the measured hot water. Pour the liquid over the pudding.

5 Bake the pudding for 30 minutes or until the liquid has sunk to the bottom and the cake is well-risen and springy to the touch. Sprinkle with confectioners' sugar and serve at once.

Nutty chocolate pudding
Add ½ cup chopped pecans or walnuts to the dry ingredients in step 1.

Magic lemon pudding

SERVES 4

Ingredients

4 tbsp butter, softened, plus extra for greasing

grated zest and juice of 1 large lemon

½ cup granulated sugar

2 large eggs, separated

¼ cup all-purpose flour

¾ cup milk

lemon or lime slices to decorate

SPECIAL EQUIPMENT

2-cup baking dish

Method

1 Preheat the oven to 325°F (160°C). Put the butter, lemon zest, and sugar into a bowl and beat together until pale and fluffy.

2 Add the egg yolks, flour, and lemon juice, and stir to combine. Gradually stir in the milk until evenly mixed.

3 Whisk the egg whites until stiff but not dry. Gradually fold into the lemon mixture.

4 Lightly butter the baking dish. Pour the lemon mixture into the dish and put the dish into a roasting pan. Add enough hot water to the roasting pan to come almost to the rim of the dish. Bake for 40 minutes or until the cake feels springy. Serve hot, decorated with lemon or lime slices. Leftovers are good cold.

 Cook's know-how

This "magic" pudding separates during cooking to form a cake topping with a tangy lemon sauce beneath.

Bread & butter pudding

 SERVES 6

Ingredients

12 thin slices of white bread, crusts removed

about 9 tbsp butter, softened, plus extra for greasing

1 cup mixed dried fruit

grated zest of 2 lemons

⅔ cup dark brown sugar

2½ cups milk

2 large eggs

SPECIAL EQUIPMENT

6-cup baking dish

Method

1 Preheat the oven to 350°F (180°C). Spread one side of each slice of bread with a thick layer of butter. Cut each slice of bread in half diagonally. Lightly butter the baking dish and arrange 12 of the triangles, buttered-side down, in the bottom of the dish.

2 Sprinkle with half of the dried fruit, lemon zest, and sugar. Top with the remaining bread, buttered-side up. Sprinkle with the remaining fruit, lemon zest, and sugar.

3 Beat together the milk and eggs and strain over the bread. Leave for 1 hour so that the bread can absorb some of the liquid.

4 Bake for about 40 minutes until the bread slices on the top of the pudding are a golden brown color and crisp, and the custard mixture has set completely. Serve at once.

Special occasion desserts

Cherry cheesecake

 CUTS INTO 8 SLICES

Ingredients

GRAHAM CRACKER CRUST

1¼ cups graham crackers, crushed

6 tbsp butter, melted

2 tbsp dark brown sugar

FILLING

12oz (375g) full-fat cream cheese

½ cup granulated sugar

2 large eggs, beaten

a few drops of vanilla extract

1 tbsp lemon juice

TOPPING

1 tsp arrowroot

1 x 14oz (400g) can
pitted black cherries

1 tbsp kirsch

SPECIAL EQUIPMENT

9in (23cm) springform cake pan

Method

1 Preheat the oven to 350°F (180°C). Make the graham cracker crust: mix together the crushed graham crackers, melted butter, and sugar, and press evenly over the bottom and up the sides of the cake pan.

2 Make the filling: put the cream cheese into a bowl and beat until smooth. Add the granulated sugar and beat until well-blended. Add the eggs, vanilla extract, and lemon juice. Mix until smooth and creamy.

3 Pour the filling into the graham cracker crust. Bake for 25–30 minutes until just set. Let cool completely, then transfer to the refrigerator and let chill.

4 Make the topping: dissolve the arrowroot in a little of the cherry juice. Put the cherries and their juice into a small pan and add the arrowroot mixture with the kirsch. Bring to a boil, stirring, until thick. Let cool completely.

5 Spoon the cherries on top of the cheese filling. Chill. Use a knife to loosen the side of the cheesecake from the pan, then remove the cheesecake. Serve chilled.

Rich **fruit** Christmas **cake**

 CUTS INTO ABOUT 30 SLICES

Ingredients

2½ cups currants

1½ cups golden raisins

1½ cups raisins

1½ cups glacé cherries, quartered, rinsed, and dried

1 cup dried apricots, sliced into small pieces

⅓ cup mixed candied peel, coarsely chopped

¼ cup brandy, plus extra for soaking

2⅓ cups all-purpose flour

1 tsp ground pumpkin pie spice

½ tsp grated nutmeg

21 tbsp soft butter, plus extra for greasing

1⅓ cups dark brown sugar

5 large eggs

¼ cup whole unblanched almonds, coarsely chopped

1 tbsp blackstrap molasses

finely grated zest of 1 large lemon

finely grated zest of 1 large orange

SPECIAL EQUIPMENT

deep 9in (23cm) round or 8in (20cm) square cake pan

Method

1 Combine the fruit and candied peel in a large bowl. Add the brandy and stir to mix well. Cover and leave overnight.

2 Preheat the oven to 275°F (140°C). Put the remaining ingredients into a large bowl and beat well with an electric mixer until thoroughly blended. Stir in the soaked fruits and any liquid.

3 Grease the cake pan with butter, line the bottom and sides with a double layer of parchment paper, and grease the paper. Spoon the mixture into the prepared pan. Level the surface and cover the top of the cake with parchment paper.

4 Bake for 4¾–5 hours until firm to the touch and a skewer inserted into the middle of the cake comes out clean. Let the cake cool in the pan.

5 When the cake has cooled, pierce it in several places with a fine skewer and pour in a little brandy. Remove the cake from the pan, but leave the lining paper on. Wrap the cake in more parchment paper, then overwrap with foil. Store the cake in a cool place for up to 3 months to mature, unwrapping and spooning over more brandy (1–2 tbsp) occasionally.

6 Decorate the cake with glacé fruit, almond paste, or ready-to-use icing (see p170). Tie a ribbon around the cake, if wished.

Opposite, clockwise from top:
Candied fruit cake (p170), Snow white cake (p170).

Marzipan
(almond paste)

Ingredients

2¼ cups ground almonds

1 cup granulated sugar

2 cups confectioners' sugar, sifted, plus extra for dusting

6 drops of almond extract

about 4 large egg yolks, or 2 whole eggs

Method

1 Mix the ground almonds in a bowl with the two different types of sugar until evenly combined. Lightly beat together the extract and egg yolks or whole eggs. Add almost all of this mixture to the dry ingredients and mix together until a stiff paste forms; it is best to do this with your hands. Add the remaining egg if needed so that the mixture comes together well.

2 Dust a flat surface lightly with confectioners' sugar, turn the mixture onto it, and knead with your hands to make a stiff paste. Be careful not to over-knead or the paste will be oily. Wrap in plastic wrap and store in the refrigerator until required.

Royal icing

Ingredients

2 large egg whites

5 cups confectioners' sugar, sifted

4 tsp lemon juice

Method

1 Whisk the egg whites in a large bowl lightly with a fork until bubbles begin to form on the surface. Add about half the confectioners' sugar and all of the lemon juice and beat well with a wooden spoon for about 10 minutes until brilliant white.

2 Gradually stir in the remaining confectioners' sugar until the consistency is just right for spreading or piping. If not using immediately, keep the bowl covered with a damp cloth to prevent the icing from drying out.

Cake decorations

Whichever cake you choose, you need to melt and sieve about ¼ cup apricot jam before you apply any of the decorations or icing. The jam prevents the cake from drying out and suppresses any crumbs.

Candied fruit cake

This looks most dramatic if it is made in a square pan. Brush the jam over the top of the cake and then arrange nuts and whole or sliced candied fruits and peel in a decorative pattern while the jam is still warm and sticky. Glaze with more jam and leave until set firmly in place before tying a ribbon around the sides of the cake.

Snow white cake

Brush the jam over the top and sides of the cake. Roll out the marzipan and use it to cover the cake completely, then smooth it in place with your hands and trim off any excess. Let the marzipan dry out for a few days before covering with royal icing. Use a palette knife to rough up the icing into peaks, immediately after you have spread it all over the cake. If you are using store-bought decorations for the top of the cake (here, silver dragées and fresh cranberries), you need to gently press them in before the icing sets hard.

Rich
fruit cake

 CUTS INTO 10 SLICES

Ingredients

16 tbsp soft butter or margarine, plus
extra for greasing

1 cup light brown sugar

4 large eggs

1¾ cups self-rising flour

1½ cups raisins

1½ cups golden raisins

¾ cup glacé cherries, halved
and rinsed

½ tsp ground pumpkin pie spice

1 tbsp brandy

SPECIAL EQUIPMENT

deep 8in (20cm) round cake pan

Method

1 Preheat oven to 275°F (140°C). Lightly grease the pan and line the bottom with parchment paper.

2 Combine all the ingredients in a large bowl and mix well until combined. Turn the mixture into the prepared cake pan and level the surface.

3 Bake for 2–2¼ hours. Cover the top of the cake with foil after about 1 hour to prevent the top from becoming too brown.

4 When cooked, the cake should be firm to the touch and a fine skewer inserted in the middle of the cake should come out clean. Let the cake cool in the pan before turning out. Store in an airtight container.

Hot chocolate soufflé

 MAKES 4

Ingredients

4oz (125g) dark chocolate

2 tbsp water

1¼ cups milk

3 tbsp butter, plus extra for greasing

⅓ cup all-purpose flour

2–3 drops of vanilla extract

¼ cup granulated sugar

4 large egg yolks

5 large egg whites

sifted confectioners' sugar for dusting

SPECIAL EQUIPMENT

4 x 8oz (300 ml) soufflé dishes

Method

1 Place a baking sheet in the oven and preheat the oven to 375°F (190°C). Break the chocolate into pieces and put into a small saucepan with the meaured water and a few tablespoons of the milk. Heat gently, whisking, until the chocolate has melted. Add the remaining milk, whisking to blend.

2 Melt the butter in a pan, add the flour, and cook, whisking, for 1 minute. Remove from the heat and gradually add the chocolate and milk mixture, whisking until smooth before adding more milk. Stir in the vanilla extract and granulated sugar and let cool.

3 Beat the egg yolks into the cooled chocolate mixture. Lightly butter the individual soufflé dishes and set aside.

4 Whisk the egg whites until stiff but not dry. Fold 1 large spoonful of the egg whites into the chocolate mixture, then carefully fold in the remainder. Divide the mixture among the 4 soufflé dishes.

5 Place on the hot baking sheet and bake for 30 minutes in the lower third of the oven until the soufflés are well-risen and firm. Dust with sifted confectioners' sugar. Serve the soufflés at once.

Summer berry soufflés

 MAKES 6

Ingredients

14oz (400g) frozen mixed summer berries

1 heaping tbsp cornstarch

2 tbsp cassis (black currant liqueur)

butter for greasing

3 extra large egg whites

⅔ cup granulated sugar

SPECIAL EQUIPMENT

6 x 5½oz (150ml) soufflé dishes

Method

1 Measure half of the berries into a saucepan and heat gently for a few minutes until the fruit is soft.

2 Put the cornstarch and cassis into a small bowl and mix until smooth. Add a little of the hot berry juices to the cornstarch mix, stir, and pour back into the saucepan. Heat, stirring, until thickened, then press through a sieve into a bowl, leaving just the seeds behind in the sieve. Set the berry purée aside to cool.

3 Put a baking sheet in the oven, and preheat the oven to 375°F (190°C). Butter the soufflé dishes.

4 Put the egg whites into a large bowl, and beat with a hand-held mixer on high speed until stiff but not dry. Add half of the sugar a teaspoon at a time, and keep beating until stiff and shiny. Stir a little of the whites into the berry purée, then carefully fold in the remainder until evenly combined.

5 Spoon the mixture into the prepared dishes, level the tops, then run a knife inside the rim of each dish—this will ensure that the soufflés rise evenly. Place the dishes on the hot baking sheet and bake for 8–10 minutes until the soufflés are well-risen and light golden on top.

6 Meanwhile, make a compote: heat the remaining berries and sugar in a pan over low heat, stirring until the sugar has dissolved and the fruit has defrosted. Check for sharpness and add a little more sugar if the fruit does not taste sweet enough.

7 Serve the soufflés as soon as they come out of the oven with the warm compote.

These individual soufflés look impressive and, despite their rather complicated-sounding name, are extremely simple to make.

Twice-baked lemon **soufflés**

 MAKES 6

Ingredients

butter for greasing

3 large eggs, separated

⅔ cup granulated sugar

2½ tbsp cornstarch

finely grated zest of 2 large lemons

juice of 1 large lemon

9oz (250g) low-fat cream cheese, softened

1 large tbsp lemon curd

LEMON SAUCE

¾ cup heavy cream

1 tbsp lemon curd

finely grated zest and juice of 1 lemon

SPECIAL EQUIPMENT

6 x (5fl oz/150ml) ramekins

8in (20cm) ovenproof dish

Method

1 Preheat the oven to 375°F (190°C). Grease the ramekins and line the bottoms with a disc of parchment paper. Put the egg yolks and half the sugar into a large mixing bowl and beat with a hand-held mixer until pale, thick, and frothy.

2 Mix the cornstarch, lemon zest, and lemon juice in a bowl until smooth. Fold in the egg-yolk mixture, then beat in the cream cheese and lemon curd with a spatula.

3 Beat the egg whites with a hand-held mixer until they resemble clouds. Whisking constantly, add the remaining sugar a teaspoon at a time until the whites are stiff and shiny.

4 Carefully fold the egg-white mixture into the mixing bowl, then spoon into the ramekins. Run a knife around the edge of each one to make sure they rise evenly. Set the ramekins snugly in a roasting pan, then pour in enough boiling water to come halfway up the sides of the pan.

5 Bake for 15–20 minutes or until the soufflés have risen well and are just cooked. Set aside to cool completely. Increase the oven temperature to 400°F (200°C).

6 Turn the soufflés out of the ramekins, remove the paper bases, and arrange snugly in one layer in the dish.

7 To make the sauce, put all the ingredients into a mixing bowl and whisk until smooth. Pour the sauce around the soufflés in the dish, then bake for 15–20 minutes or until bubbling and lightly browned. Serve at once.

Pavlova with pineapple & ginger

 SERVES 6–8

Ingredients

4 large egg whites

1 cup granulated sugar

1½ tsp cornstarch

1½ tsp white wine vinegar

TOPPING

1½ cups heavy or whipping cream

⅓ cup candied ginger in syrup, cut into matchstick-thin strips

1 x 14oz (400g) can pineapple rings, drained

Cook's know-how

Keep the oven door closed when you leave the meringue to dry out, but if you have a convection oven, you should leave the door slightly open. The meringue base can be made a day in advance and kept in an airtight container in a cool place until needed. Add the cream and fruit topping just before serving.

Method

1 Preheat the oven to 325°F (160°C). Draw a 9in (23cm) circle on a sheet of nonstick parchment paper, turn the paper over, and use it to line a baking sheet.

2 Beat the egg whites with a hand-held electric mixer on maximum speed until stiff, then add the sugar, 1 tsp at a time, beating the mixture constantly.

3 Blend the cornstarch and vinegar and beat into the egg white mixture.

4 Spread the mixture inside the circle on the parchment paper, building the sides up so that they are higher than the middle. Place in the oven, then immediately reduce the heat to 300°F (150°C).

5 Bake the meringue for 1 hour or until firm to the touch. Turn off the oven and leave the meringue inside for another hour.

6 Peel the parchment paper from the meringue and transfer the meringue to a serving plate. Let cool.

7 Before serving, whip the cream until stiff and stir in half of the candied ginger strips. Spoon the mixture into the middle of the meringue. Top with the pineapple rings and the remaining candied ginger strips.

You don't get successful pavlovas if you use more than six egg whites at one time, which is why I make them in two batches for this party pyramid. It is the most spectacular dessert you'll ever make.

Party **pavlova** pyramid

 SERVES 35–40

Ingredients

2 x 6 large egg whites

2 x 1¾ cups granulated sugar

2 x 1 tsp white wine vinegar

2 x 1 tsp cornstarch

FILLING

6 cups heavy cream

16oz (500g) tub full-fat Greek yogurt

2lb (900g) strawberries, hulled

1lb 10oz (750g) raspberries

1lb (450g) blueberries

a few mint leaves to decorate (optional)

Method

1 Preheat the oven to 325°F (160°C). Make a first batch of pavlova by putting six egg whites into a mixing bowl and beating with a hand-held mixer until they look like clouds. Gradually add the sugar a little at a time, beating on maximum speed until they are stiff and glossy. Mix the vinegar and cornstarch in a cup until smooth, then beat into the egg whites.

2 Line a baking sheet with parchment paper and spread the pavlova mixture out—it should be about 12in (30cm) in diameter and about 2in (5cm) thick. This will be the base for the pyramid. Slide into the oven, then immediately reduce the temperature to 250°F (120°C) and bake for 1 hour. Turn the oven off and leave the pavlova inside for an hour or overnight to dry.

3 Prepare a second batch of pavlova mixture in the same way. Use to make one pavlova measuring 10in (25cm) in diameter, another measuring 8in (20cm) in diameter, and a third that is 5in (12cm) in diameter. The smallest one can be fairly thin and should fit on a baking sheet with the 8in (20cm) pavlova.

4 Put the 10in (25cm) pavlova in the oven and bake for 15 minutes, then pop the two smaller pavlovas in as well and bake for another 45 minutes. Switch off the oven and let dry out for an hour or overnight.

5 To assemble, whip the cream until just stiff and mix with the yogurt. Place the largest pavlova on a foil-covered board or pan (it needs to be sturdy), then cover with whipped cream and half the fruit. Make sure the fruit can be seen around the edges, so the pyramid will look attractive.

6 Place the next-largest pavlova on top and cover with cream and fruit. Continue in the same way with the other pavlovas. Finish with the last of the cream and a pretty arrangement of fruit and mint leaves on top, if using. To serve, cut in wedges, starting from the top.

Pear and ginger is one of my all-time favorite combinations. This pavlova is sprinkled with pomegranate seeds just before serving—they look so pretty and glisten like little gems.

Pear & ginger pavlova

 SERVES 6

Ingredients

3 large egg whites

⅔ cup granulated sugar

1 tsp cornstarch

1 tsp white wine vinegar

TOPPING

5 fairly ripe pears, peeled, cored, and chopped into chunky slices

juice of ½ lemon

¼ cup granulated sugar

1¼ cups heavy cream, whipped

½ cup candied ginger, coarsely chopped

1 small pomegranate

Method

1 Preheat the oven to 325°F (160°C). Beat the egg whites with a hand-held mixer until they look like clouds. Gradually add the sugar a little at a time, beating on maximum speed until the whites are stiff and glossy. Mix the cornstarch and vinegar in a cup until smooth, then stir into the pavlova mixture.

2 Line a baking sheet with parchment paper and draw an 8 x 12in (20 x 30cm) rectangle on it. Spread the pavlova mixture out into the rectangle with a knife, then create a well in the middle by building up the sides.

3 Slide the baking sheet into the oven, immediately reduce the temperature to 250°F (120°C), and bake for 1 hour. Turn the oven off and leave the pavlova in the oven for another hour to dry out.

4 To make the topping, put the pears, lemon juice, and sugar into a small pan and barely cover with water from the tap. Simmer gently over low heat for 10 minutes or until the pears are just tender. Leave in the liquid until needed, then drain, reserve a few for decoration, and stir the rest into the whipped cream with the ginger.

5 Arrange the pavlova on a serving plate, spoon the cream into the well, and decorate with the reserved pears. Cut the pomegranate in half, pick out the seeds, and sprinkle over the top. Serve at room temperature.

Meringue roulade is such a classic dessert. As a twist, I've added chopped roasted hazelnuts to give a lovely, nutty flavor that goes sublimely well with raspberries and cream.

Hazelnut **meringue** **roulade** with berries

 SERVES 8–10

Ingredients

sunflower oil for greasing

4 large egg whites

1 cup granulated sugar

⅓ cup toasted hazelnuts, chopped

FILLING

1¼ cups heavy cream, whipped

7oz (200g) fresh raspberries

SPECIAL EQUIPMENT

9 x 13in (22 x 33cm) Swiss roll pan

Method

1 Preheat the oven to 400°F (200°C). Lightly oil the Swiss roll pan and line with a sheet of parchment paper. Meanwhile, put the egg whites into a large clean bowl and beat with a hand-held mixer on full speed until very stiff. With the mixer still on full speed, gradually add the sugar a teaspoon at a time, beating well between each addition. The meringue is ready when it is glossy and very, very stiff.

2 Spread the mixture into the prepared pan and sprinkle with the hazelnuts. Bake for 8 minutes or until lightly golden. Reduce the temperature to 325°F (160°C) and bake for another 20 minutes.

3 Remove the meringue from the oven and turn hazelnut-side-down onto a sheet of parchment paper. Remove the paper from the base of the meringue and let cool for 10 minutes.

4 Spread the whipped cream over the meringue and scatter with the raspberries. Using the parchment to help you, roll the meringue up fairly tightly from one of the long ends to form a roulade. Wrap in parchment paper and chill well before serving.

5 To serve, unwrap and cut into slices.

Strawberry meringue roulade

 SERVES 8

Ingredients

sunflower oil for greasing

4 large egg whites

1 cup granulated sugar

½ cup sliced almonds

confectioners' sugar for dusting

FILLING

1¼ cups heavy or whipping cream, whipped until thick

8oz (250g) strawberries, quartered

SPECIAL EQUIPMENT

9 x 13in (23 x 33cm) Swiss roll pan

Method

1 Preheat the oven to 400°F (200°C). Lightly oil the Swiss roll pan and line with parchment paper.

2 Whisk the egg whites until stiff but not dry. Add the sugar, 1 tsp at a time, and continue to whisk until all the sugar has been incorporated and the mixture is stiff and glossy.

3 Spoon the meringue into the lined pan and tilt to level the surface. Sprinkle with the sliced almonds.

4 Bake near the top of the oven for about 8 minutes until the top is golden brown.

5 Reduce the oven temperature to 325°F (160°C) and continue baking for 10 minutes or until the meringue is firm to the touch.

6 Remove the meringue from the oven and turn onto a sheet of parchment paper. Peel the lining paper from the base and let the meringue cool for 10 minutes.

7 Spread the whipped cream evenly over the meringue and scatter the strawberries over the cream.

8 Roll up the meringue from a long side, using the lining paper to help lift it. Wrap the roulade in parchment paper and let chill in the refrigerator for about 30 minutes. Lightly dust with sifted confectioners' sugar before serving.

The ultimate chocolate **roulade**

 SERVES 8

Ingredients

butter for greasing

6oz (175g) dark chocolate, broken into pieces

6 extra large eggs, separated

⅔ cup granulated sugar

2 tbsp cocoa powder, sifted

1¼ cups heavy or whipping cream

confectioners' sugar for sifting

SPECIAL EQUIPMENT

9 x 13in (23 x 33cm) Swiss roll pan

Method

1 Preheat the oven to 350°F (180°C). Lightly grease the pan, then line with parchment paper, pushing it into the corners.

2 Put the chocolate into a heatproof bowl. Place the bowl over a pan of hot water, and heat gently until the chocolate has melted, stirring occasionally. Remove the bowl from the pan and allow the chocolate to cool slightly until warm.

3 Put the egg whites into a large bowl and beat with a hand-held mixer on high speed until stiff but not dry. Put the sugar and egg yolks into another large bowl, and beat with the same mixer (no need to wash) on high speed until light, thick, and creamy. Add the chocolate to the egg yolk mixture and stir until blended.

4 Fold 2 large spoonfuls of the egg whites into the chocolate mixture, then carefully fold in the remaining egg whites followed by the cocoa powder. Turn into the prepared pan, and gently level the surface.

5 Bake for 20–25 minutes until risen. Remove from the oven and let the cake cool in the pan (it will dip and crack a little).

6 When the cake is cold, whip the cream in a bowl until it just holds its shape. Sift confectioners' sugar over a large sheet of parchment paper. Turn the cake onto the paper with one of the short edges facing you and peel off the lining paper. Spread the whipped cream over the cake, then make a shallow cut through the cream and cake along the short edge nearest to you, about ¾in (2cm) in from the edge. Roll up the roulade away from you, tightly to start with, and using the paper to help. Don't worry if it cracks—this is quite normal, and how it should be. Sift confectioners' sugar over the roulade before serving.

Fresh fruit baskets

 MAKES 8

Ingredients

4 large egg whites

1 cup granulated sugar

1 cup heavy cream

berries and mint sprigs (optional) to decorate

SAUCE

8oz (250g) fresh or frozen raspberries

2 tbsp confectioners' sugar

a squeeze of lemon juice to taste

Piping meringue baskets

Draw 8 x 4in (10cm) circles on nonstick parchment paper; turn over. Spoon the meringue into a piping bag fitted with a medium star nozzle and pipe inside the circles, building up the sides to form baskets.

Method

1 Preheat the oven to 250°F (120°C) and line a baking sheet with parchment paper. Beat the egg whites in a scrupulously clean large bowl with a hand-held blender on maximum speed, until the whites are stiff and look like clouds.

2 Keeping the mixer on maximum speed, add the granulated sugar a teaspoon at a time and continue whisking until the mixture is stiff and shiny.

3 Make the raspberry sauce: purée the raspberries in a blender or food processor, then push the purée through a sieve with a spoon into a bowl (discard the seeds in the sieve). Stir in the sugar and lemon juice to taste. Chill in the refrigerator until ready to use.

4 Pipe 8 meringue baskets (see box, below). Bake for 1–1½ hours until firm. Let cool.

5 Whip the cream until it forms stiff peaks. Fill the baskets with the cream, top with berries, and decorate with mint sprigs if you like. Serve with the chilled raspberry sauce.

Chocolate meringue shells

 MAKES 12

Ingredients

4 large egg whites

1 cup granulated sugar

2oz (60g) dark chocolate, chopped

GANACHE

4oz (125g) dark chocolate, chopped

½ cup heavy cream

Piping meringue shells

Spoon the meringue into a piping bag fitted with a medium star nozzle. Pipe 24 even-sized shells, about 2in (5cm) in diameter at the base, onto nonstick parchment paper.

Method

1 Preheat the oven to 250°F (120°C) and line a baking sheet with parchment paper. Beat the egg whites in a scrupulously clean large bowl with a hand-held blender on maximum speed, until the whites are stiff and look like clouds.

2 Keeping the mixer on maximum speed, add the granulated sugar a teaspoon at a time and continue whisking until the mixture is stiff and shiny.

3 Pipe 24 shells (see box, below left). Bake for 1–1½ hours until firm. Let cool. Put the chocolate into a heatproof bowl over a pan of hot water and heat until melted. Drizzle over the meringues and let set.

4 Make the ganache: put the chopped chocolate and the cream into a heavy-bottomed saucepan and heat gently, stirring occasionally, until the chocolate has melted.

5 Remove the pan from the heat and whisk the ganache for about 5 minutes until the mixture is fluffy and cooled. Sandwich the meringues together with the chocolate ganache.

Mocha meringue mille-feuilles

 MAKES 6

Ingredients

MERINGUE

4 large egg whites

1 cup sugar

1 cup sliced almonds

confectioners' sugar for dusting

COFFEE CHANTILLY CREAM

1 cup heavy cream

1 tsp instant coffee, dissolved in 1 tbsp water

2–3 tbsp caster sugar

Method

1 Preheat the oven to 250°F (120°C). Beat the egg whites in a scrupulously clean large bowl with a hand-held mixer on maximum speed until the whites are stiff and look like clouds.

2 Keeping the mixer on maximum speed, add the granulated sugar a teaspoon at a time and continue beating until the mixture is stiff and shiny.

3 Spoon 18 mounds of meringue onto nonstick parchment paper, then spread them flat with a palette knife until they are very thin and about 3in (7.5cm) in diameter. Sprinkle with the almonds, reserving a few for decoration. Bake for 1–1½ hours until firm. Cool.

4 Make the coffee Chantilly cream: whip the cream until it forms soft peaks. Add the coffee and sugar to the cream and whip until stiff peaks form.

5 Sandwich the meringue discs together in threes, with the coffee Chantilly cream in between. Dust with a little confectioners' sugar and a few leftover almonds before serving.

Opposite, clockwise from top left:
Mocha meringue mille-feuilles, Chocolate meringue shells (p187), Fresh fruit baskets (p186).

Index

Index entries in *italics* refer
to techniques

A

all-in-one cakes 10
almonds
  Almond tuiles 74
  Apple strudel 130
  Christmas pudding 154
  Coconut macaroons 82
  Danish pastries 32
  Dundee cake 141
  French apricot & almond pie 106
  Heavenly chocolate cake 36
  Mincemeat & almond tart 92
  Mocha meringue
    mille-feuilles 188
  Pink almond macaroons 80
  Plum & almond tart 116
  Rich fruit Christmas cake 168
  Strawberry meringue roulade 182
  Tropical tartlets 119
apples
  Apple strudel 130
  Apple tarte au citron 108
  Blackberry & apple cobbler 128
  Classic apple crumble 125
  Double-crust apple pie 98
  Eve's pudding 148
  French apple tart 102
  Mini apple, apricot & hazelnut
    crumbles 124
  Spiced Eve's pudding 148
  sweetening 125
  Tarte tatin 100
apricots
  Apricot & almond galette 122
  Apricot & cherry loaf cakes 31
  Apricot upside-down pudding 49
  Crunchy apricot crumble 126
  Danish pastries 32
  Figgy seeded bites 137
  French apple tart 102
  French apricot & almond pie 106
  Mini apple, apricot & hazelnut
    crumbles 124
  Pineapple upside-down cake 49
  Rich fruit Christmas cake 168
  Tropical tartlets 119

B

Bakewell tart 144
Baklava 60
bananas
  Banoffi pie 146
  Cherry & banana loaf 28
  Fruity banana bread 30
Banoffi pie 146
bars
  Chocolate and mint bars 84
  Figgy seeded bites 137
  Flapjacks 18
  Gingerbread 88
  Iced lime bars 84
  Iced orange & lemon bars 86
Battenburg cake 48
beets: Chocolate & beet cake 38
Best-ever brownies 87
Blackberry & apple cobbler 128
blueberries
  Blueberry & vanilla muffins 22
  Blueberry puffs 120
  Party pavlova pyramid 178
blackstrap molasses
  Gingerbread 88
  Rich fruit Christmas cake 168
Brandy butter 154
Brandy snaps 76
Bread & butter pudding 162

C

cakes
  all-in-one 10
  Battenburg cake 48
  Chocolate & orange mousse
    cake 40
  Chocolate & beet cake 38
  creamed 10
  decorations 170
  Devil's food cake 39
  Dundee cake 141
  Heavenly chocolate cake 36
  Lemon layer cake 140
  Marbled coffee ring cake 46
  Pineapple & carrot cake 42
  Pineapple upside-down cake 49
  Rich fruit cake 171
  Rich fruit Christmas cake 168
  Simnel cake 44

Swiss roll 50
testing 11
Victoria layer cake 140
whisked 10
Wimbledon cake 138
see also loaf cakes; muffins
cake pans, preparing 10
candied peel
  Christmas pudding 154
  Dundee cake 141
  Rich fruit Christmas cake 168
  Simnel cake 44
carrots
  Christmas pudding 154
  Pineapple & carrot cake 42
cherries
  Apricot & cherry loaf cakes 31
  Cherry & banana loaf 28
  Cherry cheesecake 166
  Danish pastries 32
  Dundee cake 141
  Fruity banana bread 30
  Rich fruit cake 171
  Rich fruit Christmas cake 168
  Simnel cake 44
chocolate
  Banoffi pie 146
  Battenburg cake 48
  Best-ever brownies 87
  Chocolate & orange mousse
    cake 40
  Chocolate chip fairy cakes 51
  Chocolate cupcakes 52
  Chocolate meringue shells 187
  Chocolate and mint bars 84
  Chocolate profiteroles 64
  Chocolate whoopie pies 83
  Chooclate & beet cake 38
  Cupcake tier 58
  Devil's food cake 39
  Double-chocolate muffins 26
  Heavenly chocolate cake 36
  Hot chocolate soufflé 172
  Magic chocolate pudding 158
  Marbled coffee ring cake 46
  Mississippi mud pie 109
  Nutty chocolate pudding 158
  Pecan & chocolate chip
    cookies 71

Religieuses 63
  Ultimate chocolate roulade 184
  Viennese fingers 68
  White chocolate & strawberry
    muffins 24
Christmas cake, rich fruit 168
Christmas pudding 154
cinnamon
  Gingerbread 88
  Pineapple & carrot cake 42
  Plum crumble 126
  Spiced Eve's pudding 148
  Strawberry & rhubarb pie 94
  Zucchini loaf 27
Classic apple crumble 125
Cobbler, blackberry & apple 128
coconut
  Coconut macaroons 82
  Figgy seeded bites 137
  Pineapple & carrot cake 42
coffee
  Best-ever brownies 87
  Coffee & walnut cupcakes 56
  Coffee éclairs 62
  Double-chocolate muffins 26
  Marbled coffee ring cake 46
  Mississippi mud pie 109
  Mocha meringue mille-feuilles 188
  Pinwheel cookies 69
  Sticky toffee pudding 152
cookies
  Almond tuiles 74
  Brandy snaps 76
  Fridge cookies 70
  Ginger snaps 75
  Gingerbread Christmas cookies 72
  Pecan & chocolate chip
    cookies 71
  Pinwheel cookies 69
  Viennese fingers 68
cream cheese
  Cherry cheese cake 166
  Pineapple & carrot cake 42
  Raspberry tartlets 118
  Twice-baked lemon soufflés 175
creamed cakes 10
crème pâtissière 15
crumbles
  Classic apple crumble 125

Crunchy apricot crumble 126
Mini apple, apricot & hazelnut crumbles 124
Plum crumble 126
Rhubarb & ginger crumble 126
Crunchy apricot crumble 126
cupcakes
　Chocolate cupcakes 52
　Coffee & walnut cupcakes 56
　Cupcake tier 58
　decorating 58
　glacé 58
　Lemon cupcakes with lemon frosting 54

D

Danish pastries 32
　shaping 14
dates
　Date & walnut loaf 28
　Sticky toffee pudding 152
desserts, special occasion
　Cherry cheesecake 166
　Chocolate meringue shells 187
　Fresh fruit baskets 186
　Hazelnut meringue roulade with berries 181
　Hot chocolate soufflé 172
　Mocha meringue mille-feuilles 188
　Party pavlova pyramid 178
　Pavlova with pineapple & ginger 176
　Pear & ginger pavlova 180
　Strawberry meringue roulade 182
　Summer berry soufflés 174
　Twice-baked lemon soufflés 175
　Ultimate chocolate roulade 184
Devil's food cake 39
Devon scones 134
Double-chocolate muffins 26
Double-crust apple pie 98
dried fruit
　Apple strudel 130
　Apricot & cherry loaf cakes 31
　Bread & butter pudding 162
　Christmas pudding 154
　Dundee cake 141
　Fruity banana bread 30
　Rich fruit cake 171
　Rich fruit Christmas cake 168

Simnel cake 44
Spiced Eve's pudding 148
Welsh cakes 136
Dundee cake 141

E F

Eve's pudding 148
Fairy cakes 51
figs: Figgy seeded bites 137
Flapjacks 18
French apple tart 102
French apricot & almond pie 106
French pancakes 20
Fresh fruit baskets 186
Fridge cookies 70
frosting 11
　chocolate 11, 38, 52, 64
　coffee 56, 62
　fudge 36, 38
　glacé 58
　lemon 54
　spreading 11
Fruity banana bread 30

G H I

ginger
　Apricot upside-down pudding 49
　Ginger snaps 75
　Gingerbread 88
　Gingerbread Christmas cookies 72
　Pavlova with pineapple & ginger 176
　Pear & ginger pavlova 180
　Rhubarb & ginger crumble 126
golden (corn) syrup
　Brandy snaps 76
　Figgy seeded bites 137
　Flapjacks 18
　Ginger snaps 75
　Pecan pie 110
　Treacle pudding 150
　Treacle tart 142
greasing 10
hazelnuts
　Crunchy apricot crumble 126
　Hazelnut meringue roulade with berries 181
　Mini apple, apricot & hazelnut crumbles 124

Heavenly chocolate cake 36
honey: Baklava 60
Hot chocolate soufflé 172
Iced lime bars 84
Iced orange & lemon bars 86
icing
　ornamental 72
　Royal icing 170

K L

Key lime pie 114
lemons
　Apple tarte au citron 108
　Bread & butter pudding 162
　Iced orange & lemon bars 86
　Lemon cupcakes with lemon frosting 54
　Lemon meringue pie 112
　Lemon layer cake 140
　Magic lemon pudding 160
　St. Clement's apple pie 98
　Tarte au citron 104
　Treacle tart 142
　Twice-baked lemon soufflés 175
limes
　Iced lime bars 84
　Key lime pie 114
lining 10
loaf cakes
　Apricot & cherry loaf cakes 31
　Cherry & banana loaf 28
　Date & walnut loaf 28
　Fruity banana bread 30
　Zucchini loaf 27

M N O

macaroons
　Coconut macaroons 82
　Pink almond macaroons 80
Magic chocolate pudding 158
Magic lemon pudding 160
Marbled coffee ring cake 46
marzipan see almond paste
meringue
　Chocolate meringue shells 187
　drying out 176
　Fresh fruit baskets 186
　Hazelnut meringue roulade with berries 181

Lemon meringue pie 112
Mocha meringue mille-feuilles 188
Party pavlova pyramid 178
Pavlova with pineapple & ginger 176
Pear & ginger pavlova 180
Queen of puddings 149
Strawberry meringue roulade 182
Mincemeat & almond tart 92
Mini apple, apricot & hazelnut crumbles 124
Mississippi mud pie 109
Mocha meringue mille-feuilles 188
muffins
　Blueberry & vanilla muffins 22
　Double-chocolate muffins 26
　White chocolate & strawberry muffins 24
nuts see almond paste; almonds; hazelnuts; pecan nuts; walnuts
Nutty chocolate pudding 158
oats
　Classic apple crumble 125
　Crunchy apricot crumble 126
　Figgy seeded bites 137
　Flapjacks 18
oranges
　Chocolate & orange mousse cake 40
　Iced orange & lemon bars 86
　Orange fairy cakes 51
　St. Clement's apple pie 98
　Tropical tartlets 119

P

Pancakes, French 20
Party pavlova pyramid 178
passion fruit: Wimbledon cake 138
pastries
　Apple strudel 130
　baking blind 13
　Baklava 60
　Blueberry puffs 120
　Chocolate profiteroles 64
　choux 13
　Coffee éclairs 62
　Danish pastries 32
　quick puff 12
　Religieuses 63

shortcrust 13
see also pies & tarts
pâte sucrée 12
Pavlova with pineapple & ginger 176
peaches: Blueberry puffs 120
Pear & ginger pavlova 180
pecan nuts
  Nutty chocolate pudding 158
  Pecan & chocolate chip cookies 71
  Pecan pie 110
pies & tarts
  Apple tarte au citron 108
  Apricot & almond galette 122
  Bakewell tart 144
  Banoffi pie 146
  Double-crust apple pie 98
  French apple tart 102
  French apricot & almond pie 106
  Key lime pie 114
  Lemon meringue pie 112
  Mincemeat & almond tart 92
  Mississippi mud pie 109
  Pecan pie 110
  Plum & almond tart 116
  Raspberry tartlets 118
  Royal raspberry tart 96
  St. Clement's apple pie 98
  Strawberry & rhubarb pie 94
  Tarte au citron 104
  Tarte tatin 100
  Treacle tart 142
  Tropical tartlets 119
pineapple
  Pavlova with pineapple

& ginger 176
Pineapple & carrot cake 42
Pineapple upside-down cake 49
Pink almond macaroons 80
Pinwheel cookies 69
plums
  Plum & almond tart 116
  Plum crumble 126
puddings
  Apricot upside-down pudding 49
  Bread & butter puddings 162
  Christmas pudding 154
  Eve's pudding 148
  Magic chocolate pudding 158
  Magic lemon pudding 160
  Nutty chocolate pudding 158
  Queen of puddings 149
  Spiced Eve's pudding 148
  Steamed jam pudding 156
  Sticky toffee pudding 152
  Treacle pudding 150
  see also desserts, special occasion

Q R

Queen of puddings 149
raspberries
  Bakewell tart 144
  Fresh fruit baskets 186
  Hazelnut meringue roulade with berries 181
  Party pavlova pyramid 178
  Pink almond macaroons 80
  Queen of puddings 149
  Raspberry tartlets 118
  Royal raspberry tart 96
  Swiss roll 50

Victoria layer cake 140
Religieuses 63
rhubarb
  Rhubarb & ginger crumble 126
  Strawberry & rhubarb pie 94
Rich fruit cake 171
Rich fruit Christmas cake 168
Rosewater fairy cakes 51
roulades
  Hazelnut meringue roulade with berries 181
  Strawberry meringue roulade 182
  Ultimate chocolate roulade 184
Royal icing 170
Royal raspberry tart 96

S T

St. Clement's apple pie 98
sauces, puddings 15
Shortbread 78
Simnel cake 44
soufflés
  Hot chocolate soufflé 172
  Summer berry soufflés 174
  Twice-baked lemon soufflés 175
Spiced Eve's pudding 148
Steamed jam pudding 156
steamed puddings 14
Sticky toffee pudding 152
strawberries
  Party pavlova pyramid 178
  Queen of puddings 149
  Strawberry & rhubarb pie 94
  Strawberry meringue roulade 182
  Victoria layer cake 140
  White chocolate & strawberry

muffins 24
Wimbledon cake 138
Summer berry soufflés 174
Swiss roll 50
Tarte au citron 104
Tarte tatin 100
tarts see pies & tarts
Treacle pudding 150
Treacle tart 142
Tropical tartlets 119
Twice-baked lemon soufflés 175

U V W

Ultimate chocolate roulade 184
Victoria layer cake 140
Viennese fingers 68
walnuts
  Baklava 60
  Best-ever brownies 87
  Coffee & walnut cupcakes 56
  Date & walnut loaf 28
  Fridge cookies 70
  Fruity banana bread 30
  Nutty chocolate pudding 158
  Pineapple & carrot cake 42
  Sticky toffee pudding 152
  Zucchini loaf 27
Welsh cakes 136
whisked cakes 10
White chocolate & strawberry muffins 24
Whoopie pies, chocolate 83
Wimbledon cake 138

Z

Zucchini loaf 27

Acknowledgments

Author's acknowledgments: A huge thank you goes to Lucy Young, my assistant of 25 years for her dedication to this book. Liaising with the publishers is down to her. She also wrote some of the recipes with me. I thank you Lucy, for your work and friendship. Big thanks to Lucinda McCord who tested the recipes to make them foolproof—we discuss, taste, and discuss some more to make them foolproof. And many thanks also to our recipe editor Jeni Wright, the food photographers William Shaw and Bill Reavell, the cover photographer Georgia Glynn Smith, and the creative team at DK Publishing.

DK's acknowledgments: Designer Alison Shackleton; Editors Christy Lusiak and Elizabeth Yeates; Senior Editor Margaret Parrish; Pre Production Producer Andy Hilliard; Senior Producer Stephanie McConnell; Senior Jacket Creative Nicola Powling; Image Retoucher Steve Crozier; Special Sales Creative Project Manager Alison Donovan; Art Director Maxine Pedliham; Publishing Director Mary-Clare Jerram; Culinary Consultant Kate Curnes-Ramos; Executive Acquisitions Editor Lori Hand; Proofreader Christine Heilman; Recipe tester Jan Stevens; Indexer Marie Lorimer.